US Light Cruise in action

By Al Adcock

Color by Don Greer

Illustrated by Richard Hudson and Ernesto Cumpian

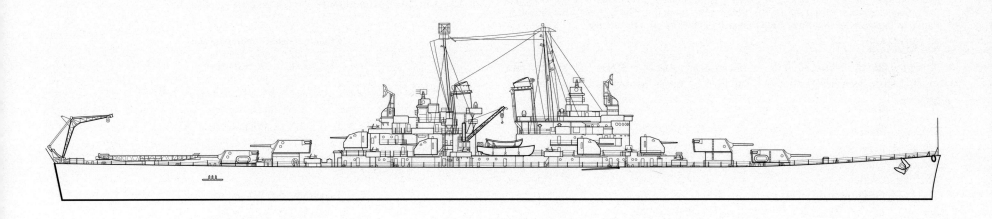

Warships Number 12

squadron/signal publications

(Cover) The USS CLEVELAND races through gentle ocean swells shortly after her commissioning in mid-1942. The CLEVELAND and her sisters arrived just in time to replace the cruiser losses suffered during the Solomons Campaign. The CLEVELAND is camouflaged in Measure 22 — a Navy Blue hull and Haze Gray superstructure.

Credits

All of the photographs used in this publication are official U S Navy or shipyard photos that have been declassified and supplied by the following individuals or photo archives:

Real War Photos
Elsilrac Enterprises
National Archives
Floating Drydock
Todd Shipbuilding and Drydock
Navy of Chile

Acknowledgments:

I want to thank the following individuals for going the extra nautical mile for me on this project: Ms. Maja Larson, Public Relations, Todd Shipbuilding; Bob Carlisle, owner of Elsilrac Enterprises; George Chizmar, owner of Real War Photos; H. Patrick Hreachmack, author of various publications on World War II camouflage; and last, but certainly not least, Tom Walkowiak of The Floating Drydock. Without your valued help my task would have been almost impossible!

ISBN 0-89747-407-4

If you have any photographs of aircraft, armor, soldiers or ships of any nation, particularly wartime snapshots, why not share them with us and help make Squadron/Signal's books all the more interesting and complete in the future. Any photograph sent to us will be copied and the original returned. The donor will be fully credited for any photos used. Please send them to:

Squadron/Signal Publications, Inc.
1115 Crowley Drive
Carrollton, TX 75011-5010

Если у вас есть фотографии самолётов, вооружения, солдат или кораблей любой страны, особенно, снимки времён войны, поделитесь с нами и помогите сделать новые книги издательства Эскадрон/Сигнал ещё интереснее. Мы переснимем ваши фотографии и вернём оригиналы. Имена приславших снимки будут сопровождать все опубликованные фотографии. Пожалуйста, присылайте фотографии по адресу:

Squadron/Signal Publications, Inc.
1115 Crowley Drive
Carrollton, TX 75011-5010

軍用機、装甲車両、兵士、軍艦などの写真を所持しておられる方はいらっしゃいませんか？どの国のものでも結構です。作戦中に撮影されたものが特に良いのです。Squadron/Signal社の出版する刊行物において、このような写真は内容を一層充実し、興味深くすることができます。当方にお送り頂いた写真は、複写の後お返しいたします。出版物中に写真を使用した場合は、必ず提供者のお名前を明記させて頂きます。お写真は下記にご送付ください。

Squadron/Signal Publications, Inc.
1115 Crowley Drive
Carrollton, TX 75011-5010

(Right) The USS SAVANNAH (CL-42) comes along side the escort carrier USS SANTEE (CVE-29) in the South Atlantic in January of 1943. Both SAVANNAH and SANTEE, in concert with their escorting destroyers, were combing the Atlantic searching for German raiders. SAVANNAH — a BROOKLYN class cruiser — is camouflaged in Measure 22. (Floating Drydock)

42

3

Introduction

The ideas that brought about cruiser designs were developed during the 1600s when it became apparent that trade ships would need protection from marauding pirates. These new ships, known as frigates, were up-gunned and carried a full rig of sails. Conceivably, any ship they could not outrun, they could outfight. By the beginning of the 19th Century, frigates roamed the world's oceans in search of pirates and — perhaps just as often — other frigates.

During the transition period of the late 1800s, two types of cruisers were being constructed: 'protected' and 'armored'. The British were the first to construct a protected cruiser — HMS ESMERALDA. The protected cruiser carried both belt (side) and deck armor, while the armored cruiser carried only deck armor. By the beginning of World War I, most cruisers under construction were of the armored type.

The first US ships to be classified as cruisers were the WAMPANOAG class of the Federal Navy during the American Civil War (1861-1865). The WAMPANOAG class were built of wood and powered by both sail and steam. The sails provided a long range, while the steam provided speed and maneuverability. This combination gave the cruisers the choice of fighting or retiring to engage at a more advantageous time.

The ATLANTA and BOSTON were the first all steel cruisers built for the US Navy. These ships were built and launched during the mid-1880s and designated 'protected cruisers' since they carried both side and deck armor. The BOSTON and ATLANTA, in common with most large warships of the time, were powered by sails and coal-fired steam. Despite the US Navy being convinced of the practicality of steam-powered ships, the lack of coaling stations around the world dictated a ship design that used the wind for a proportion of its propulsion. Both ves-sels were built of the finest materials available at the time; the ATLANTA served until 1912 and the BOSTON, serving as a receiving ship named DISPATCH (IX-2), served until 1946.

The US Navy authorized the purchase of two cruisers from Brazil in 1898. They had been built by the Armstrong Company of Great Britain, but were never taken into service by the Brazilian Navy. The NEW ORLEANS and ALBANY were both armed with six 6-inch guns and displaced 3450 tons (3129.8 MT). They were designated light cruisers CL-22 and 23 when the 'CL' designation came into use. Both ships were sold in 1930.

Following the Washington Naval Conference of 1922, cruisers were limited to 10,000 standard tons (9072 MT) and 8-inch (203 MM) guns. During the London Conference of 1930, a new class of cruiser was created — the light cruiser. These ships were limited to 10,000 tons, while the guns were limited to 6.1 inches (155 MM). The heavy cruisers retained their previous displacement and gun limits. The conference essentially created an 'A' (or heavy) cruiser and a 'B' or light cruiser. The designator 'CA' for heavy cruiser was the result, although 'CL' was used for light cruisers ('CB' was later used for the ALASKA (CB-1) class battle cruisers).

The first US Navy vessels designated light cruisers were the CHESTER (CS-1) class (the 'C' was for cruiser, while the 'S' was for Scouting). The class, eventually redesignated 'CLs', consisted of the CHESTER, BIRMINGHAM, and SALEM. The ships displaced 3750 tons (3402 MT) and were lightly armed with two 5-inch (12.7 CM) guns, six 3-inch (7.62 CM) guns, and two torpedo tubes. These three scouting cruisers, authorized under the 1904 Naval Act, were the first turbine engined ships in the US Fleet. In 1910, the BIRMINGHAM also became the first US naval vessel to have an aircraft take off from its deck, thus becoming (in some respects) the first US aircraft carrier. This single event would not be the last time a cruiser was used as a basis for an aircraft carrier — during World War II the hulls of CLEVELAND class light cruis-

The WAMPANOAG was the class leader of the first of four Federal Navy cruisers. Designed and launched during the Civil War, the ships were found to be unsuitable for naval operations and none saw service. The ships were powered by both steam and sail and had a top speed of 17 knots. (Elsilrac)

The ATLANTA and her sister BOSTON were the first iron ships built for the US Navy. The ATLANTA was commissioned in 1886 and was armed with two 8-inch/30 (20.32 CM) main guns and six 6-inch/30 (15.24 CM) guns in her secondary battery. The ATLANTA was brig rigged since sail power was still used for emergencies. (Elsilrac)

ers were used to construct the INDEPENDENCE (CVL-22) class light carriers.

The beginning of the First World War found the US Navy equipped with many obsolete armored and protected cruisers which saw little service during that conflict. The US was mainly involved with convoy protection and anti-submarine patrols. The US Navy authorized the construction of a new class of light cruiser, then known as Scouting Cruisers, in 1916. The scouting cruiser would have the capability of achieving 30 plus knots, enough to keep up with the destroyers and battle cruisers of the day. The new cruisers were designated the OMAHA class. Construction began in 1918 — too late to see service during the First World War.

Light cruisers served as flagships for various cruiser and submarine Battle Forces in the Atlantic, Pacific, and Asiatic fleets. Their larger size allowed them to provide quarters and communications facilities for flag officers and their staffs.

US light cruisers were named for cities in the United States and its territories, as well as to commemorate previous US ships. The names of some of the decommissioned light cruisers would also grace some of the new heavy cruisers that were built between the two world wars.

Over the years, light cruisers have worn various paint schemes or camouflage measures ranging from white to black to many colors in between. At the turn of the century, US Navy ships were painted white, thus the name of the 'Great White Fleet'. When the OMAHA class became operational in the mid-1920s, the standard scheme of light gray was applied. This light gray scheme, known as Measure 3, was applied to most US naval vessels up to the middle of 1940. During WW I, 'dazzle' or 'piebald' schemes, composed of various colors and geometric patterns, were devised to confuse a surface observer.

The surface oriented dazzle schemes worked quite well during the First War, since little in the way of aerial attacks occurred. This lack of an aerial threat was also reflected in the fact that few anti-aircraft (AA) weapons were carried aboard ship. By the beginning of the Second World War, however, a need for protection from air attack had been amply demonstrated. Several different schemes were tried. The most commonly used US Navy scheme, Measure 22, consisted of Navy Blue and Haze Gray. This camouflage was designed as a compromise scheme for hindering both surface and air observation.

Measure 21, the overall Navy Blue System, was found to provide the best protection from aerial observers and was widely used in the Pacific Theater. The measure consisted of an overall application of Navy Blue (5-N) paint on all horizontal and vertical surfaces. Ships wearing this scheme were sometimes referred to as 'Blue Beetles'. Measure 21 was employed from 1942 to 1945.

Measure 12, employed from 1941 to 1943, consisted of a graded system of Sea Blue (5-S), Ocean Gray (5-O), and Haze Gray (5-H). This scheme, or variations of it, was often combined with gray or green splotches, sometimes with widely varying degrees of artistic license. Both the ATLANTA (CL-51) and JUNEAU (CL-52) wore Measure 12, but their splotch patterns were completely different.

All of the light cruisers carried, or were fitted to carry, an aviation unit except the ATLANTA-OAKLAND class — they were considered too small for aircraft and catapults. (A single aircraft could be carried in place of a ship's boat and hoisted aboard using the boat crane.) Shipboard aviation units were used to spot gunfire for the main armament and provide scouting for the ship to locate enemy fleets. The development and use of search and fire control radars gradually eliminated the floatplane mission. Cruiser aviation units were referred to as Cruiser Scouting Squadrons (VSO). Their presence was not always popular with the crews since they took up valuable space both above and below deck. Additionally, the stored avia-

The VESUVIUS was classified as a 'dynamite cruiser' and armed with three 15-inch (38.1 CM) pneumatic guns that were aimed by pointing the ship at the target. The guns fired a 980 pound (444.5 KG) shell of which 500 lbs (226.8 KG) was dynamite. VESUVIUS displaced 980 tons (889 MT) — the lightest of all US cruisers. (Real War photos)

The RALEIGH (C-8) was classified as a 'protected cruiser' and equipped with armored decks and hull sides. RALEIGH was the only sister to the class leader CINCINNATI (C-7). Both cruisers were armed with one 6-inch/40 main gun and 10 5-inch/40 broadside cannons. The RALEIGH was commissioned in 1894 and served until 1921. (Real War Photos)

US Light Cruiser Development

OMAHA Class

ATLANTA Class

BROOKLYN Class

CLEVELAND Class

ST LOUIS Class

WORCESTER Class

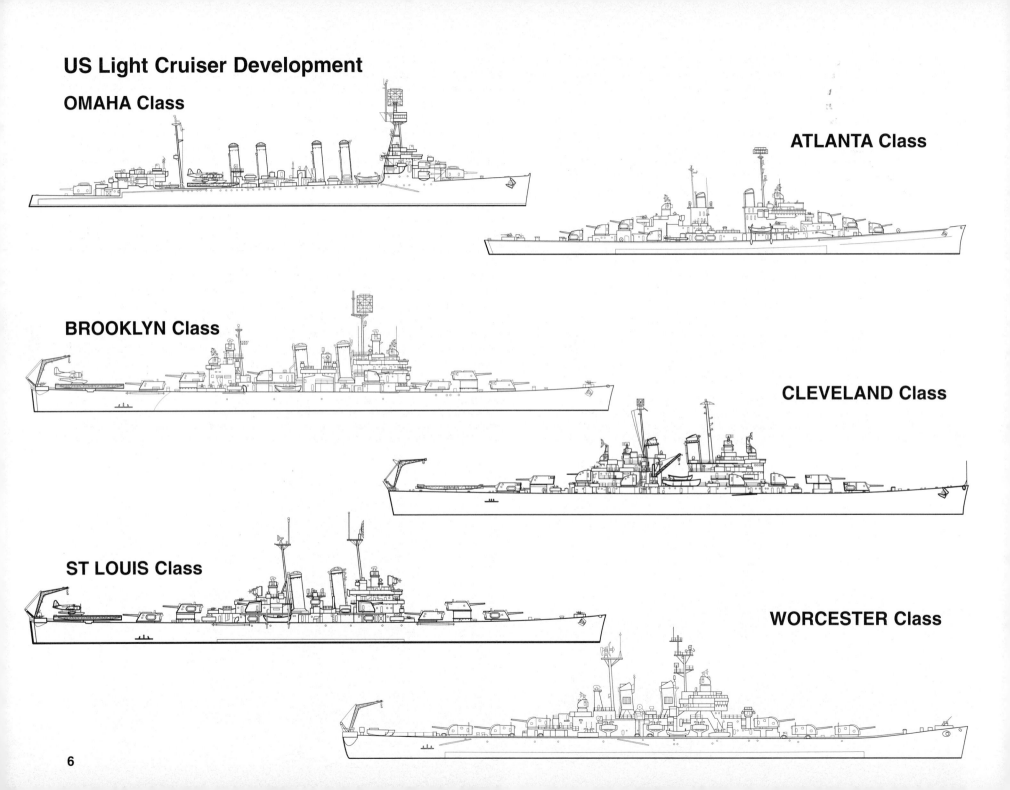

tion gas presented a constant fire hazard. The catapult locations varied by class. OMAHA's two catapults were located on the deck aft of the number four funnel, while the remaining 13 classes had their catapults on the after deck. The number and type of aircraft also varied by class and year with the most common being the Vought-Sikorsky OS2U Kingfisher and the Curtiss/NAF SOC/SON Seagull. The Curtiss SO3C Seagull I/Seamew was briefly used aboard the ST LOUIS (CL-49) and BILOXI (CL-80) during 1943, but was found to be inadequate as a scout floatplane. In 1945, the Curtiss SC-1 Seahawk entered service, although its tenure was brief. By 1950, fixed wing aircraft were no longer assigned to US Navy cruisers.

Light cruiser main and secondary armaments varied widely by class and, during the war, often from ship to ship. The OMAHA class carried 6-inch/53 guns, while the BROOKLYN, ST LOUIS, CLEVELAND, and WORCESTER classes were armed with 6-inch/47 guns and the ATLANTA-OAKLAND classes were fitted with the 5-inch/38 anti-aircraft guns. Secondary armament, designed to protect the ship from enemy aircraft and provide some anti-ship and shore bombardment capability, ranged from .50 caliber machine guns up to 5-inch/38 caliber guns. All weapons were optically sighted until radar sets began being fitted in the early 1940s.

Twenty-one inch torpedo tubes were fitted to the OMAHA and ATLANTA-OAKLAND classes, but these were rarely used in combat. Depth charges were also among the armament found on the ATLANTA-OAKLAND class and on a few of the OMAHAs as well — notably the RICHMOND (CL-9). The OMAHAs were also originally equipped to lay mines, however, this capability was deleted following unsuccessful trials in 1924.

The only electronic equipment carried by early light cruisers were the long and short band radios used to communicate with the fleet. Air and surface search radars became the norm on all light cruisers by 1942. The most common air search sets were the SK and SC, while the surface search sets were the SL, SU, and SG radars. Shipboard radar was one of the major advantages held by the US during the war in the Pacific.

Three US Navy light cruisers were lost in WW II — all in the Pacific. The ATLANTA (CL-51) was sunk by Japanese gunfire and torpedoes during the Solomons Campaign on 13 November 1942. The JUNEAU (CL-52) was torpedoed twice on 13 December 1942 with the loss of all but 10 (out of over 700) of her crew. The third loss was the HELENA (CL-50), sunk by three Japanese 'Long Lance' torpedoes during the Battle of Kula Gulf on 6 July 1943. The losses, quite low in comparison to the numbers that were placed in harm's way, followed the loss of several US heavy cruisers (CA) during the early days of the Pacific War.

US Navy light cruisers served admirably during the Second World War with most earning one or more Battle Stars for their service. The ATLANTA was awarded a Presidential Unit Citation for her gallantry during the Battle of Guadalcanal. The CLEVELAND (CL-55), SANTA FE (CL-60), and MONTPELIER (CL-57) were the most highly decorated light cruisers with 13 Battle Stars each and Navy Unit Commendations for their service in the Second World War. Two CLEVELAND class cruisers also served during the Vietnam Conflict. The TOPEKA (CL-67) and OKLAHOMA CITY (CL-91) both served to protect the fleet as Guided Missile Cruisers (CLG). The TOPEKA earned three Battle Stars and the OKLAHOMA CITY earned 13 Battle Stars for their service off the coast of Vietnam.

Six CLEVELAND class light cruisers were converted to Guided Missile Cruisers (CLG) during 1959 to 1961. The conversions consisted of removing some of the main battery 6-inch guns and replacing them with either TALOS or TERRIER surface to air missile (SAM) systems. The conversions included increased crew space and, in some instances, increased command and control spaces for Flag Officers.

The US Navy found itself at a distinct disadvantage at the beginning of the Pacific War; most of its battleships were either sunk or seriously damaged at Pearl Harbor. The heavy cruisers took over much of the battleship role, leaving the light cruisers to serve in the heavy cruiser role. The light cruisers took up the gauntlet and served with great distinction during the long march to the Japanese home islands.

The ALBANY and her sister NEW ORLEANS were purchased from Brazil in 1898. Brazil had originally purchased the two cruisers from Great Britain. The ALBANY was armed with six 6-inch/50 US guns and three 18-inch (45.7 cm) torpedo tubes. Both the ALBANY and NEW ORLEANS served until 1930. (Elsilrac)

The BIRMINGHAM (CS 2) and her two sisters, CHESTER (CS 1 and class leader) and SALEM (CS 3), were the first 'scout cruisers'. The BIRMINGHAM, equipped with a temporary flight deck on her forecastle, served as the US Navy's first aircraft carrier for Eugene Ely's flight off her deck on 14 November 1910. (Elsilrac)

OMAHA Class

The OMAHA class were the first modern cruisers ordered by the US Navy since the CHESTER class. OMAHA was ordered on 26 December 1916 and construction began at the Todd Shipbuilding and Drydock at Tacoma, Washington on 6 December 1918. The OMAHA was launched on 14 December 1920 and following her commissioning, joined the fleet in 1923. A full seven years and an expenditure of eight million dollars had elapsed from her order to her commissioning.

The ten ships of the OMAHA class scout cruisers had the lines of — and closely resembled — the US Navy's World War I 'flush deck' destroyers with their four stacks and long lean lines. There the similarity ended. The OMAHAs were 555 feet, 6 inches (169.3 M) in length and had a beam of 55 feet, 4 inches (16.9 M). Standard displacement was rated at 7050 tons (6395.7 MT), while their war load rating was 9700 tons (8799.8 MT) with a mean draft of 20 feet (6.09 M). Eight Yarrow boilers provided 90,000 shaft horsepower for the four Westinghouse turbines. The four screws generated speeds up to 35 knots. With 1986 tons (1801.7 MT) of fuel, the OMAHAs had a range of 6800 miles (10,943.2 KM) at 15 knots.

The OMAHA class was protected by 1.5 inches (38 MM) of deck armor and three inches (76 MM) of belt armor. The turrets were lightly armored with less than .5 inches (12.7 MM) of steel to protect the 6-inch (152 MM) guns.

The OMAHAs were originally equipped with 12 6-inch/53 caliber guns in their main battery. The guns were mounted in pairs in single fore-and-aft turrets, while the remaining eight weapons were mounted in single casemates in the superstructure. Operations at sea proved the number 5 and 6 guns (the two lower guns in the aft superstructure) to be extremely wet. Most were removed during refits, although the MARBLEHEAD carried a single 6-inch gun mounted in a casemated turret on the centerline of her aft superstructure during the mid-to-late 1930s. By the beginning of World War II, the main armament had been reduced to 10 — in some cases eight — 6-inch guns. The reduction was designed to reduce top weight and allow the installation of new radars and fire control equipment to the superstructure and masts.

Secondary armament originally consisted of two 3-inch/50 caliber dual purpose guns, one of each mounted on the fore and aft superstructure. This armament was later increased to eight by the beginning of the war with six of these weapons being mounted along the main deck amidships. In addition to the 3-inch/50 guns, .50 caliber machine guns were used for anti-aircraft protection. Oerlikon 20 MM cannons, having increased range and hitting power, eventually replaced the .50 caliber machine guns when they became available. By 1942, the 1.1-inch, four barrel heavy machine gun had been added to increase anti-aircraft protection. The 1.1-inch gun, known as the 'Chicago Piano', was found to be prone to jamming and difficult to keep in service. This weapon was replaced by the Bofors 40 MM gun when supplies became available.

The OMAHA class cruisers were completed with two triple and two twin 21-inch (533 MM) trainable torpedo tubes. The triple tubes were placed singularly on each side of the deck just forward of the aft superstructure, while the twin tubes were mounted on the upper hull side main deck just forward of the deck mounted tubes. The hull-mounted tubes were removed before the war in an attempt to save top weight and to ease concerns of them taking on water. Over the course of the war, the triple tubes in a few of the scouts, notably the CINCINNATI, were removed in favor of additional 40 MM AA weapons.

Depth charge roller tracks were added to the stern of RALEIGH (CL-7), RICHMOND (CL-9), CONCORD (CL-10), and presumably TRENTON (CL-11) since they all served in the Northern Pacific in the Aleutian and the Kurile Islands. To be effective sub hunters, sonar, hydrophones, and a high frequency direction finding (HF/DF) antenna would surely have been used as well. The depth charges are believed to have been the MK 6 and 8 'ashcan' and MK 9 and 14 fast sinking types.

As designed, the OMAHAs were to have the capability of laying mines. The mines were to be stored in the aft superstructure and launched via mine tracks running back to the stern. This installation, however, was never used operationally following unsuccessful tests in 1924.

When the OMAHAs were built, the electronic equipment consisted of short wave radios. These radios required an extensive array of wire antennas mounted on high masts. Prior to the introduction of radar, the main armament was optically sighted through range finders mounted on the roof of the fore and aft superstructure. When fire control radars became available, these were installed atop the foremast and on an auxiliary mast aft of the main mast. The FC fire control radar was used to direct the main armament. SK, SC, and CXAM-1 antennas and sets were used for air search, while SL and SU sets and antennas were fitted for detecting surface targets.

By 1925, the Vought UO-1 floatplanes were assigned to the OMAHA class cruisers. Two trainable catapults were mounted on the quarter deck between the number 4 stack and the aft superstructure. An aircraft handling crane was fitted to facilitate aircraft loading and recovery. The catapults used gunpowder charges to launch the aircraft.

Three shipyards were involved in the construction of the OMAHA class. Seattle Construction and Drydock (Todd Shipbuilding and Drydock) of Tacoma, Washington constructed the OMAHA (CL-4), MILWAUKEE (CL-5), and CINCINNATI

The class leader OMAHA (CL-4) moves at 25 knots during one of her post-commissioning shakedown cruises in 1923. The OMAHA was built by Todd Shipbuilding and Drydock (ex-Seattle Shipbuilding and Drydock) in Tacoma, Washington. The OMAHA was armed with twelve 6-inch guns. Tall masts and an extensive array of aerials were needed for the early radio sets. (Todd Shipbuilding)

(CL-6). Bethlehem Shipbuilding Company of Quincy, Massachusetts built the RALEIGH (CL-7) and DETROIT (CL-8), while William Cramp and Sons of Philadelphia, Pennsylvania completed the RICHMOND (CL-9), CONCORD (CL-10), TRENTON (CL-11), MARBLEHEAD (CL-12), and MEMPHIS (CL-13).

All of the OMAHA class cruisers won Battle Stars for their actions during World War II, except the MEMPHIS and MILWAUKEE. MEMPHIS was used for training, while the MILWAUKEE engaged in convoy escort and patrol duties in the Caribbean Sea, South Atlantic, and the South Pacific until loaned to the Soviet Navy in 1944. The MILWAUKEE was renamed MUR-MANSK during her five year tour with the Soviet Navy and was used in the North Atlantic escorting convoys from the US to the Soviet Union. The DETROIT was the most highly decorated of the scout cruisers earning six Battle Stars for her actions in the North Pacific and off Iwo Jima and Okinawa.

When the Japanese attacked Pearl Harbor on 7 December 1941, RALEIGH (CL-7) and DETROIT (CL-8) were among the many cruisers docked in the harbor. The DETROIT escaped unhurt. She was assigned to Task Force One and charged with finding the Japanese Fleet following the attack. The RALEIGH, however, was the first ship struck by a Japanese torpedo. Shortly thereafter, RALEIGH was hit by a bomb. Severely damaged and listing to port, only heroic efforts by the RALEIGH's crew and harbor personnel managed to save the ship. The RALEIGH was repaired, refitted, and sent out to join the fleet and fight in the Northern Pacific.

When World War II began, the elderly OMAHA class light cruisers were widely regarded as second class vessels ready for retirement — most had been in service for 15 years. Pearl Harbor changed that way of thinking. The US Navy needed every ship that could be mustered — and that included the old scout cruisers.

OMAHA Class Light (Scout) Cruiser

The MILWAUKEE (CL-5) was the second ship in the OMAHA class and like her sister, was constructed by Todd in Tacoma. The MILWAUKEE had a cruising range of 3000 miles (4827.9 KM) at 30 knots. The blacked out area below the main mast is the portal for the twin starboard main deck mounted torpedo tubes. (Todd Shipbuilding)

The MILWAUKEE was camouflaged in Measure 12 with splotches in January of 1942. The main battery on the MILWAUKEE was reduced to ten 6-inch guns in order to increase the anti-aircraft battery. The MILWAUKEE (CL-5) was turned over to the Soviet Navy in 1944, renamed MURMANSK, and given a gray paint scheme. (Real War Photos)

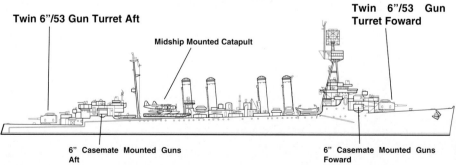

Twin 6"/53 Gun Turret Aft

Midship Mounted Catapult

Twin 6"/53 Gun Turret Foward

6" Casemate Mounted Guns Aft

6" Casemate Mounted Guns Foward

(Above) Naval Aircraft Factory VE-7Hs sit on their aircraft handling dollies on MILWAUKEE's catapult deck. The port side triple torpedo tubes are just aft the catapult. The VE-7H was later replaced by the Curtiss SOC/SON and the Vought OS2U. The aircraft were used to observe and correct the ship's gunfire. (Real War Photos)

(Below) The CINCINNATI (CL-6) wore a Measure 12 scheme with splotches in 1942. The main mast carries CXAM-1 radar, while the tripod foremast is fitted with FC fire control and SG-1 radar. Splinter shields have been erected around the 5-inch mid-ship anti-aircraft guns. The CINCINNATI was also armed with two 1.1-inch (2.8 CM) anti-aircraft guns — one fore and one aft — at this time. (Floating Drydock)

(Above) CINCINNATI shows off her increased anti-aircraft suite on the aft superstructure. Two of the aft mounted six-inch guns were removed to increase AA protection. A movie screen has been erected on the number four funnel in anticipation of viewing the latest Betty Grable movie. (Floating Drydock)

10

The damaged RALEIGH (CL-7) lists to port while being supported by yard craft following the attack on Pearl Harbor on 7 December 1941. The RALEIGH is camouflaged in Measure 1. The RALEIGH survived to serve in the Aleutian Islands until 1944. The RALEIGH earned three Battle Stars for her actions in the Pacific. (Real War Photos)

The RALEIGH moves out of Mare Island Navy Yard following her overhaul in 1942. The overhaul was necessary due to the torpedo and bomb damage inflicted on her during the Japanese attack on Pearl Harbor. The RALEIGH now wears Measure 21 — the overall Navy Blue scheme. (Floating Drydock)

OMAHA Class Weapons

The RALEIGH was camouflaged in Measure 32/1D — consisting of light gray and black — in May of 1944. Her defensive armament was increased with the addition of 40MM and 3-inch (7.62 CM) guns. All of the air and sea search radar antennas are now mounted on the foremast. (Real War Photos)

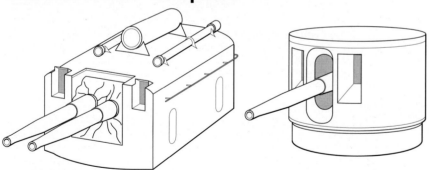

6-inch/53 Gun Turret

6-inch/53 Casemate Gun

3-inch/50 Anti-Aircraft Gun

.50 Caliber Anti-Aircraft Gun

(Above) The CONCORD (CL-10) shows off her newly increased defensive armament consisting of additional 5-inch, 3-inch, 1.1-inch, and 20 MM guns. Censors have deleted the radar antennas from the masts. The CONCORD is camouflaged in Measure 22, the Graded System. The CONCORD earned one Battle star for actions off Alaska. (Floating Drydock)

(Top Left) The DETROIT (CL-8) moves out into the Pacific in August of 1942 protected by an umbrella of barrage balloons. The DETROIT is camouflaged in Measure 21, a scheme used in the South Pacific from 1942 to 1945. The DETROIT was awarded six Battle Stars for her service in the Pacific. (Floating Drydock)

(Above Left) The RICHMOND (CL-9) displays her Measure 32/3D camouflage scheme in 1944. RICHMOND won two Battle Stars for her actions in the Northern Pacific during 1943 through 1945. Both the main and foremast are fitted with air and sea search radar antennas. (Real War Photos)

(Left) The RICHMOND trains her port torpedo tubes out to the side in 1942 photo. The war time censors have retouched the radar antennas on the two masts. Two Naval Aircraft factory SON-1 scout planes from Cruiser Scouting Squadron Three (VCS-3) are on the catapults. Depth charge roller tracks have been mounted on the stern. The RICHMOND is camouflaged in Measure 21, an overall Navy Blue scheme, designed to help her blend into the water. (Real War Photos)

(Above) The CONCORD undergoes an overhaul in a Navy Yard during early 1942. She shares the wharf space with YMS minecraft, yard tugs, Destroyers (DD), an Escort Carrier (CVE), and a solitary British cruiser. Admiral R.E. Byrd used the CONCORD during a survey mission to the Southwest Pacific after her overhaul. (Floating Drydock)

(Top Right) The TRENTON (CL-11) wore a Measure 32/2F camouflage scheme in 1944 and was outfitted with FC fire control radar and additional defensive armament. She served in the North Pacific off Alaska for the majority of her career and earned one Battle Star. (Floating Drydock)

(Above Right) The MARBLEHEAD (CL-12) achieved 30 knots on run number 19 out of Cramps Shipbuilding, Philadelphia, Pennsylvania on 13 August 1924. The MARBLEHEAD was damaged during the Battle of the Java Sea and had to steam 9000 miles (14,483.7 KM) before repairs could be made in New York. Following her stint in dry-dock, MARBLE-HEAD served in both the North and South Atlantic. The MARBLEHEAD earned two Battle Stars and a Navy Unit Commendation for her wartime exploits. (Floating Drydock)

(Right) The MEMPHIS (CL-13) moves out of the New York Navy Yard and into the Atlantic on 2 November 1942. The MEMPHIS and MILWAU-KEE were the only two light cruisers not to see combat as a US Navy ship. The MEMPHIS is camouflaged in Measure 12, but without the usual splotches. (Floating Drydock)

13

BROOKLYN Class

The BROOKLYN class was authorized in 1933 as part of a plan to bring the United States up to the strength allowed under the terms of the London Naval Treaty of 1930. The BROOKLYN (CL-40) was laid down on 12 March 1935 and launched from the New York Navy Yard on 30 November 1936. Her cost was some 15 million US dollars. The 1933 authorization also included three additional light cruisers — PHILADELPHIA (CL-41), SAVANNAH (CL-42), and NASHVILLE (CL-43). The class was originally to consist of nine ships, however, the last two hulls, ST LOUIS (CL-49) and HELENA (CL-50), were separated into the ST LOUIS class due to armament, machinery, and superstructure changes.

BROOKLYN class cruisers were 608 feet, 4 inches (185.4 M) in length with a beam of 61 feet 7 inches (18.77 M) and a mean draft of 20 feet (6.10 M). Standard displacement was rated at 9700 tons (8799.8 MT), while their full war load rose to 11,580 tons (10,505.4 MT). Eight Babcock and Wilcox boilers provided steam to the four Parsons geared steam turbines. The available 100,000 shaft horsepower, driving four screws, provided a maximum speed of some 33 knots. The BROOKLYNs had a range of 7800 miles (12,552.5 KM) using 2175 tons (1973.2 MT) of fuel oil at a speed of 15 knots. Her complement consisted of 1200 officers and men.

BROOKLYN class cruisers were armored with 5-inch (12.7 CM) belts at the waterline, 6.5 inches (16.5 CM) on the turret faces, 5 inches on the conning tower, and 2 inches (5 CM) on the deck. The barbettes were protected by 6 inches (15.24 CM) of armor.

The BROOKLYN's main battery consisted of fifteen 6-inch/47 caliber Mk-16 (152 MM) guns triple mounted in five turrets — three forward and two aft. The guns had a range of 13 nautical miles (24.1 KM) and a muzzle velocity of 2700 feet (822.9 M) per second firing a 130 pound (59 KG) armor piercing high explosive round. Her secondary armament comprised eight 5-inch/25 caliber Mk 27 dual-purpose mounts that were to be used primarily for anti-aircraft protection. Close in anti-aircraft defense was originally provided by eight .50-inch (50 caliber) water cooled machine guns. This armament was increased to 16 to 20 40 MM Bofors guns in

both twin and quad mounts and up to 24 20 MM Oerlikon weapons in single and twin mounts. The number of AA weapons varied according to the ship and year.

Over the course of the war, anti-aircraft armament was dramatically increased to counter Japanese kamikazes and German glide bombs. During a mid-war refit, the SAVANNAH and HONOLULU had their 5-inch/25 mounts replaced by 5-inch/38s to increase their anti-aircraft effectiveness.

When the war began, very little electronic gear was fitted to the BROOKLYNs. The onset of the war, however, provided much impetus to the manufacture and fielding of radar search and fire control sets. These sets were fitted to the BROOKLYNs as soon as they became available. The SG and SG-1 sets were used for sea search, while the SK and SC sets were employed for air search. Radar was also provided for fire control.

BROOKLYN class cruisers were fitted with a pair of catapults on the stern along with an aircraft and cargo handling crane. The area below deck, between the squared off stern and the number five 6-inch mount, was taken up by the aircraft hangar. Hangar access was via a large sliding hatch that provided a relatively dry space for storage and maintenance. The hangar could accommodate up to eight scout planes and enough spares to construct a further two. The aircraft were brought up to the deck by an elevator. The BROOKLYNs normally embarked the Vought-Sikorsky OS2U Kingfisher or the Curtiss/NAF SOC/SON Seagull from various Cruiser Scouting Squadrons (VCS) — usually VCS-8 or VCS-9.

There were four builders of the BROOKLYN class. BROOKLYN (CL-40) and HONOLULU (CL-48) were constructed at the New York Navy Yard. The PHILADELPHIA (CL-41) was built at Philadelphia Navy Yard, Pennsylvania. SAVANNAH (CL-42), NASHVILLE (CL-43), and PHOENIX (CL-46) were constructed at New York Shipbuilding Company, Camden, New Jersey. BOISE (CL-47) was built along side the carriers YORKTOWN (CV-5) and ENTERPRISE (CV-6) at Newport News Shipbuilding and Drydock, Newport News, Virginia.

When the war began for the United States on 7 December 1941, both the HONOLULU and

The BROOKLYN (CL-40) was ordered in 1933 and was the class leader of a new generation of light cruisers. All of the BROOKLYN class were armed with fifteen 6-inch main guns in five turrets. Their secondary armament consisted of eight 5-inch anti-aircraft guns. The BROOKLYN is camouflaged in Measure 12 with splotches. (Real War Photos)

BROOKLYN Class

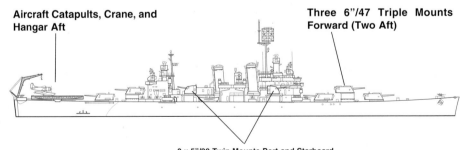

Aircraft Catapults, Crane, and Hangar Aft

Three 6"/47 Triple Mounts Forward (Two Aft)

2 x 5"/38 Twin Mounts Port and Starboard

PHOENIX were at Pearl Harbor. HONOLULU was damaged, while the PHOENIX became part of Task Force One and tasked with the futile search for the Japanese Fleet. BROOKLYN was in the Atlantic on convoy duty. PHILADELPHIA was in Boston Navy Yard for maintenance. SAVANNAH, escorting the carrier RANGER (CV-4), and NASHVILLE (operating separately) were both in the Caribbean. NASHVILLE was soon assigned to the Pacific to escort the carrier HORNET (CV-8) on the April 1942 Doolittle Raid on Japan. The BOISE was off the Philippines and was quickly pressed into service escorting convoys from the US West coast to the Pacific Islands.

The BROOKLYN class light cruisers earned a combined 49 Battle Stars during World War II. Additionally, the PHILADELPHIA and HONOLULU were each awarded a Navy Unit Commendation for their actions during the war. The NASHVILLE and BOISE each earned 10 Battle Stars. There were no losses of any BROOKLYN class cruisers, although there were a few close calls in both the Atlantic and Pacific Theatres. During the Battle of Cape Esperance in October of 1942, the BOISE was severely damaged by a large caliber Japanese projectile hit on the number one turret. The resulting explosion set off a powder magazine. While fires raged and with the ship in danger of exploding, another round opened the hull — effectively extinguishing the flames. The HONOLULU lost her bow to a torpedo during the Battle of Kolombangara in July of 1943, however, there were no crew losses. HONOLULU's luck ran out, however, during the Philippines Campaign in October of 1944. A Japanese aerial torpedo struck beneath the number 3 turret. The resulting explosion claimed the lives of 60 sailors. The SAVANNAH was damaged by a German glide bomb off Salerno, Italy in September of 1943. The bomb hit the number 3 turret and exploded in the magazines. The explosion also started a large fire and blew out the bottom of the hull. In circumstances similar to BOISE, the rapid flooding extinguished the fires. Although the SAVANNAH was saved, 197 sailors lost their lives. The NASHVILLE was struck by a Japanese kamikaze off the Philippines in December of 1944, perhaps extracting a measure of revenge for the Doolittle Raid.

The entire BROOKLYN class was placed in the reserve fleet after the war. Both HONOLULU and SAVANNAH were eventually scrapped, having suffered severe structural damage during the war. The BROOKLYN and NASHVILLE were sold to Chile in 1951 and renamed the O'HIGGINS and CAPTAIN PRAT (later CHACA BUCO) respectively. The PHILADELPHIA was sent to Brazil and named BARROSO, while the PHOENIX and BOISE went to Argentina as the 17 de OCTUBRE (later GENERAL BELGRANO) and NUEVE de JULIO. All but one of the light cruisers served their South American navies until they were again decommissioned. The one exception was the GENERAL BELGRANO — sunk by a British submarine during the Battle of the Falkland Islands in 1982.

The BROOKLYN steams out of the Philadelphia Navy Yard in 1943 carrying her new Measure 22 camouflage scheme. The cruiser spent her entire wartime career in the Atlantic and earned four Battle Stars. The BROOK-LYN was purchased by Chile in 1951 for 3.7 million dollars and renamed the O'HIGGINS. (Floating Drydock)

The PHILADELPHIA (CL-41), launched in 1936, was the second ship in the BROOKLYN class. She joined the Pacific Fleet following her commissioning. The PHILADELPHIA is camouflaged in Measure 22. Vought OS2U floatplanes from VCS-2 are secured to the two catapults. The PHILADELPHIA was turned over to the Brazilian Navy in 1951 and renamed BARROSO. (Floating Drydock)

The SAVANNAH (CL-42) was constructed by New York Shipbuilding and commissioned in 1938 and, like her two earlier sisters, joined the Pacific Fleet for workup and training. This ship earned three Battle Stars for combat in the Atlantic. The SAVANNAH was hit by a German radio-controlled glide bomb off of Salerno, Italy in September 1943. The damage was so severe that the SAVANNAH never ventured into combat again. (Floating Drydock)

(Above) The SAVANNAH uses her aircraft handling crane to load supplies at Boston Navy Yard in August of 1942. The supplies are being loaded into the hangar area and are believed to be aircraft parts. The SAVANNAH carries camouflage Measure 22, consisting of Navy Blue (5-N) and Haze Gray (5-H). (Floating Drydock)

(Below) The NASHVILLE (CL-43) hoists one of her VCS-9 Curtiss SOC scout planes aboard in 1942. The NASHVILLE escorted the carrier HORNET (CV-8) during the Doolittle Raid on Japan in April of 1942. The NASHVILLE earned 10 Battle Stars for her actions during the war in the Pacific. (Floating Drydock)

(Above) The waist mounted 5-inch/25 caliber guns used on the BROOKLYN class were dual purpose weapons, but were mainly employed in the anti-aircraft role. Splinter shields, used to protect the gun crews from shrapnel and other flying debris, were added following the outbreak of the war. (Floating Drydock)

NASHVILLE (CL-43) steams in the Pacific in 1943. The aircraft hanger hatch, at the stern between the catapults, is deployed forward under the Number Five turret. The hangar elevator is in the up position. The hangar could accommodate up to six aircraft with their wings folded. The NASHVILLE was sold to Chile and initially renamed CAPITAN PRAT. She was later christened CHACABU-CO. (Floating Drydock)

The BOISE (CL-47) steams at full power in the Atlantic off of Rockland, Maine during her Preliminary Trials on 8 July 1938. The BOISE earned ten Battle Stars for her service in both the Atlantic and Pacific theaters. In 1951, the BOISE was sold to Argentina and renamed the NUEVE de JULIO (Ninth of July). (Floating Drydock)

BROOKLYN Class Main Battery
Five Turrets — Three Forward, Two Aft

The HONOLULU (CL-48), moored at a Pacific anchorage in 1944, is camouflaged in Measure 32/2C. The HONOLULU was hit by three Japanese torpedoes during the course of her service in the Pacific. The HONOLULU was awarded 10 battle Stars for her actions in the Pacific. (Real War Photos)

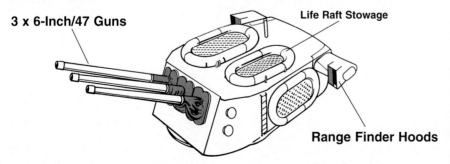

3 x 6-Inch/47 Guns

Life Raft Stowage

Range Finder Hoods

The HONOLULU steams in the Pacific off Hawaii shortly after her commissioning during 1938. She is painted in Measure 3 — an overall light gray scheme. The 5 inch/25 guns mounted at midship were replaced during the war with 5 inch/38 guns for improved performance in the anti-aircraft role. The HONOLULU was in Pearl Harbor when the Japanese attacked on 7 December 1941. She was slightly damaged, however, she was quickly repaired and assigned to convoy escort duties in the Pacific. The HONOLULU was awarded a Navy Unit Commendation for her actions during the war in the Pacific. Due to structural damage sustained during the conflict, the HONOLULU was scrapped after World War Two. Thus, she was not transferred to a South American navy as was the case with five of her sister ships. (Floating Drydock)

Catapult and Aircraft Handling Crane

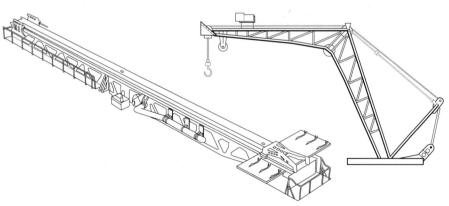

The HONOLULU lost her bow to a Japanese destroyer-launched torpedo during the Battle of Kolombangara on 13 July 1943. The cruiser was repaired with this temporary bow and sent back to the United States for permanent repairs. The HONOLULU was later hit by a Japanese aerial torpedo on 20 October 1944, suffering the loss of 60 officers and Bluejackets. (Real War Photos)

(Above) The PHOENIX (CL-46) appears in her original paint scheme of light gray — the standard US Navy ship camouflage used from 1928 until 1940. No radar antennas have been fitted to her masts at this point, however, PHOENIX would be equipped with sea and air search radars as the US approached World War Two. PHOENIX was at Pearl Harbor during the Japanese attack of 7 December 1941, however, she was not damaged and participated in a futile search for the Japanese Fleet immediately after the attack. (Elsilrac)

(Below) The PHOENIX, wearing a Measure 32/5D scheme, sails out of Philadelphia Navy Yard on 30 August 1943. Four Curtiss SOC scout planes from VCS-15 are fitted to the two catapults. Following her service with the US Navy, PHOENIX was sold to Argentina and named the 17 de OCTUBRE. She was later renamed GENERAL BELGRANO. She was sunk by the British nuclear attack submarine HMS CONQUEROR on 2 May 1982. GENERAL BELGRANO was the largest Argentinian Navy ship sunk by the British during the Battle for the Falklands. (Floating Drydock)

ST LOUIS Class

The ST LOUIS class represented the last two members of the earlier BROOKLYN class light cruisers. The ST LOUIS and HELENA were separated into a new class as a result of several differences between themselves and the seven ships in the BROOKLYN class.

The ST LOUIS class, like the BROOKLYN class, was 608 feet, 4 inches (185.4 M) in over-all length and 600 feet (182.9 M) at the waterline. Beam was 61 feet 7 inches (18.77 M) and mean draft was rated at 20 feet (6.10 M). Standard displacement amounted to 10,000 tons (9072 MT), while their full war load climbed to 12,100 tons (10,977.1 MT).

The machinery spaces were one of the differences between the BROOKLYN and ST LOUIS class cruisers. The ST LOUIS class had alternating or separated engine and boiler rooms. This arrangement was designed to reduce power losses in the event of damage to a single machin-ery compartment. Additionally, the arrangement allowed the designers to take advantage of the newer and smaller high pressure, high temperature Babcock and Wilcox boilers. These boilers provided high pressure steam for the Westinghouse geared turbines, which in turn offered 100,000 shp for the four screws. Maximum rated speed was 33.5 knots. Their steaming range at 15 knots amounted to 10,000 miles (16,093 KM) while using 2750 tons (2495 MT) of fuel oil.

The ST LOUIS' main armament and its arrangement was identical to that of the BROOKLYNs: fifteen 6inch/47 Mk 16 guns triple mounted in five turrets. The 6-inch guns had a range of 26,000 yards (23,774.4 M) with a muzzle velocity of 2500 feet (762 M) per second.

The secondary battery was another major area of difference between the BROOKLYNs and the ST LOUIS class. Eight 5-inch/38 dual-purpose guns were paired in what has been described as "roomy gunhouses". The gunhouses were a third again as large as the standard Mk32 type mount found on other light cruisers. Eight .50-inch (50 caliber) water-cooled machine guns were provided for close-in AA defense — an arrangement that was already con-sidered weak in 1939. By the end of WW II, twenty-four 40 MM Bofors cannons in twin and quad mounts were fitted, as well as up to twenty 20 MM Oerlikon weapons.

ST.LOUIS (CL-49), wearing an overall Measure 21 Navy Blue camouflage scheme, cruises in the Pacific in March of 1942. Both ST.LOUIS and her sister HELENA were modified BROOKLYN class cruisers and equipped with 5-inch guns enclosed in twin mounts. Additionally, the main mast was moved forward closer to the aft stack. The ST.LOUIS won 11 Battle Stars and the Navy Unit Commendation for her actions in the Pacific. (Floating Drydock)

Protection amounted to 5 inches (12.7 CM) of belt armor to shield the vulnerable areas of the hull, 3 inches (7.62 CM) of deck armor, and 5 inches on turret faces. The conning tower was faced with 8 inches (20.3 CM) of armor. The 5-inch turrets were faced with .75 inches (1.9 CM), while the sides were given .25 inches (.64 CM) of armor.

The ST LOUIS class cruisers also had their aft superstructure placed closer to the number 2 stack. This modification allowed the installation of two quad 40 MM AA weapons between the superstructure and the number 4 6-inch turret, thus increasing the ships' anti-aircraft defense.

Electronic equipment was sparse at the beginning of the war — only radio equipment was installed. Radar was installed when it became available in 1941. The ST LOUIS had SK-2 air search and SG sea search radars, while Identification Friend or Foe (IFF) antennas were placed on the foremast. The HELENA was fitted with SC air search and SG sea search radar. Both were fitted with MK 34 and MK 37 gun directors with radar. The MK 34 directors controlled the 6-inch main battery and the MK 37 directors were used for the dual-purpose 5-inch guns.

Two catapults were mounted at the stern for launching scout floatplanes. A single aircraft/cargo handling crane was centered at the extreme stern. The below deck hangar stor-age and maintenance arrangement was identical to that of the earlier BROOKLYN class cruis-ers. Cruiser Scouting Squadron Nine (VCS-9) was embarked aboard both the ST LOUIS and HELENA. From 1940 to early 1945, the Curtiss/Naval Aircraft Factory SOC/SON Seagull was used, however, these were replaced by the single seat Curtiss SC-1 Seahawk in 1945.

The ST LOUIS (CL-49) was ordered on 16 October 1935. The keel was laid at Newport

BROOKLYN Class

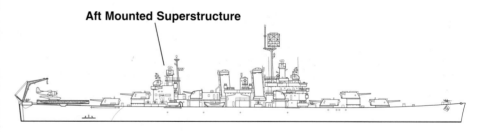

Aft Mounted Superstructure

ST LOUIS Class

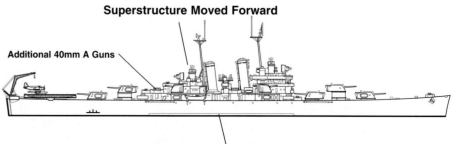

Superstructure Moved Forward

Additional 40mm A Guns

Alternating Machinery Spaces

News Shipbuilding and Drydock, Newport News, Virginia on 20 December 1936. She was launched into the James River on 15 April 1938. Following her commissioning on 19 May 1939, the ST LOUIS entered a shakedown and training period before joining the Atlantic Fleet for Neutrality Patrol. The ST LOUIS was at Pearl Harbor when the Japanese attacked. She managed to down three Japanese aircraft and stood out of the harbor with Task Force One in search of the attacking Japanese Fleet. Following duty in the Northern Pacific, the ST LOUIS fought in the Battle of Kula Gulf in July of 1943 where she lost her sister ship HELENA (also a veteran of Pearl Harbor). Less than one month later, the ST LOUIS was involved in the Battle of Kolombangara where she lost a portion of her bow to a Japanese torpedo. Following three months of repairs, the ST LOUIS was back into the fight in the Solomons. She was struck by a Japanese aerial bomb off Bougainville and suffered severe damage. Again repaired, the veteran cruiser rejoined the fight. After a much needed overhaul at Mare Island, California, the ST LOUIS was assigned to the Philippines in November of 1944. She was struck by two kamikazes, which caused enough damage to warrant a return to the US west coast for repair. ST LOUIS finished the war off the coast of Japan escorting carriers that were steadily pounding Japanese shore installations. The seven-year old cruiser was awarded 11 Battle Stars and a Navy Unit Commendation for her actions during the war.

Following World War II, ST LOUIS, like so many other ships, was put into the Reserve Fleet. The ST LOUIS was sold to Brazil in 1951 and renamed TAMADARE. She served until 1975 when she was stricken and scrapped.

The USS HELENA (CL-50) was ordered on 9 September 1935 from the New York Navy Yard, New York. Her keel was laid on 9 December 1936 — one day before the ST LOUIS. She was launched into the East River on 27 August 1938 and, following a shakedown and

training period, was commissioned on 18 September 1939. She was sent to the Pacific and was at Pearl Harbor when the Japanese attacked. A Japanese torpedo hit her amidships causing considerable damage. Temporary repairs allowed her to travel to Mare Island, California to effect permanent repairs.

While at Mare Island, HELENA's anti-aircraft armament was increased to twenty 40 MM Bofors AA weapons. These guns were supplemented by 20 MM Oerlikon cannons. HELENA headed back into the fight and joined the fleet in time for the Battle of Cape Esperance in October of 1942 where she shared in the sinking of the Japanese cruiser FURUTAKA and the destroyer FUBUKI. Following the Battle of Guadalcanal on 13 November 1942, HELENA cruised off New Georgia shelling the Japanese and covering amphibious landings.

During the night of 5-6 July 1943, the HELENA, her sister ST LOUIS (CL-49), the HONOLULU (CL-48), and four destroyers were cruising in the Kula Gulf when they engaged a force of 10 Japanese destroyers. The Japanese destroyer NIIZUKI was quickly dispatched, however, Japanese Long Lance torpedoes were already in the water and heading for HELENA. One torpedo hit the bow between turrets one and two. This hit separated the bow from the ship. Shortly thereafter, two additional torpedoes hit her amidships in rapid succession. These hits knocked out her entire engineering plant and broke her back. HELENA sank within a few minutes taking 186 sailors with her to the bottom. For this and other actions in the Pacific Theatre, HELENA was awarded seven Battle Stars and a Navy Unit Commendation.

Both the BROOKLYN and ST LOUIS classes were equipped with two catapults, and aircraft handling crane, and a below deck hangar for operating floatplanes. The ST.LOUIS class cruisers were armed with fifteen 6-inch/47 caliber guns in five triple turrets. The ST.LOUIS was sold to Brazil and renamed TAMADARE in 1951. (Floating Drydock)

By 1944, ST LOUIS was camouflaged in Measure 32/2C, the Medium Pattern System. The ST LOUIS wore this scheme for one year until repainted in Measure 21. The foremast is fitted with SK-2 air search and SG-1 sea search radar antennas. The ST LOUIS was hit by two Japanese kamikaze aircraft in 1944. (Floating Drydock)

(Below) The large squared off stern of the BROOKLYN and ST LOUIS class light cruisers housed a below deck hangar for up to six folded floatplanes. The hangar door, set into the deck between the two catapults, has been moved forward under the Number 5 turret. The secondary armament on the ST LOUIS was increased with the addition of four quad 40mm gun mounts. (Floating Drydock)

(Above) The ST LOUIS lost part of her bow to a Japanese launched torpedo during the Battle of Kolombangara. Down by the bow, the ST LOUIS was sent to Tulagi, Espirito Santo to repair her damage. On 24 August 1943, she was moored next to the repair ship VESTAL (AR-4) — also a survivor of the Japanese attack on Pearl Harbor. The repairs required three months to complete. (Floating Drydock)

Stern/Fantail Development

OMAHA Class

Pointed Stern

BROOKLYN/ST LOUIS Class

Transom Stern

Aircraft Crane

Aircraft Hangar

Catapult (P&S)

(Below) HELENA's foc'sle (forecastle) deck was covered with steel plating back to the base of the Number 1 turret. Lightly stained wood planking covered the deck further aft. This decking was later painted Deck Blue during the war. (Floating Drydock)

(Above) The HELENA (CL-50), wearing a Measure 21 Navy Blue camouflage scheme, departs Espirito Santo to join a Task Force for the fateful Battle of Kula Gulf in 1943. Two Curtiss SOC-3 observation aircraft assigned to VCS-9 are stowed on the catapults. (Floating Drydock)

(Below) The HELENA underwent a refit at Mare Island Navy Yard, San Francisco, California in early 1942. A paravane, used to fend off mines and cut their mooring cables, is stowed on the starboard main deck between Numbers 1 and 2 turrets. (Floating Drydock)

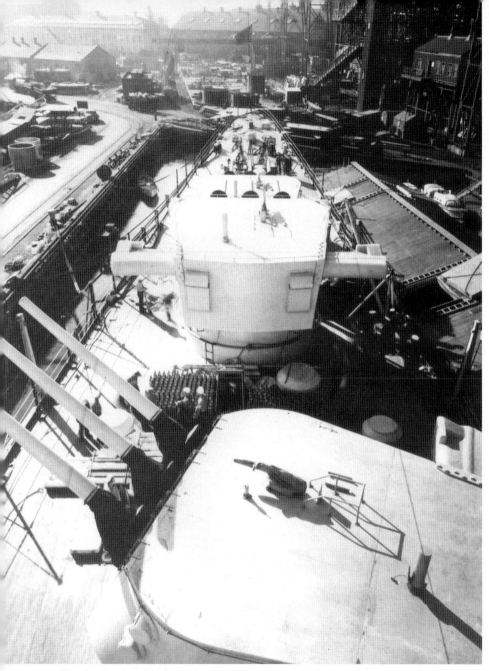

Shortly after Pearl Harbor, the HELENA was sent to San Francisco for repair and refit. Once completed, the gun crews began loading 6-inch rounds down the ammunition hatch between Turrets 2 and 3. The 6-inch guns were mounted in five triple turrets — three forward and two aft — and had a range of 26,000 yards (23,774.4 м). (Floating Drydock)

The armor plating on HELENA's Number 3 twin 5-inch mount was removed to improve maintenance access during 1942. During her extended refit, HELENA's anti-aircraft armament was increased with the addition of four quad 40 мм mounts and 20 мм single mounts for close in protection. (Floating Drydock)

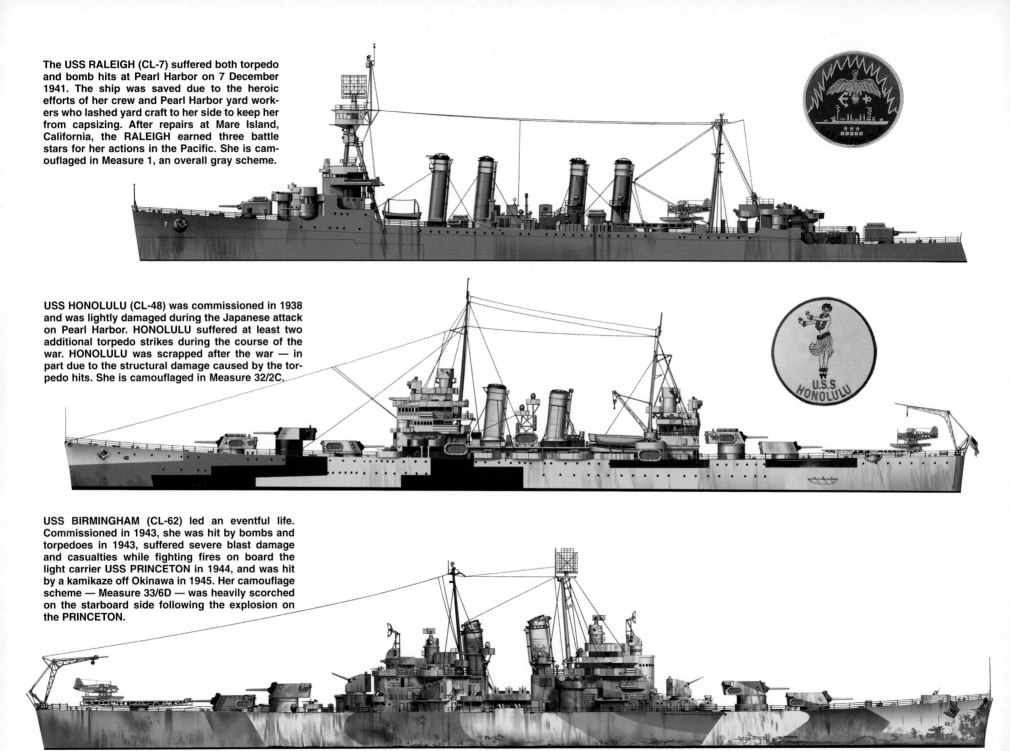

The USS RALEIGH (CL-7) suffered both torpedo and bomb hits at Pearl Harbor on 7 December 1941. The ship was saved due to the heroic efforts of her crew and Pearl Harbor yard workers who lashed yard craft to her side to keep her from capsizing. After repairs at Mare Island, California, the RALEIGH earned three battle stars for her actions in the Pacific. She is camouflaged in Measure 1, an overall gray scheme.

USS HONOLULU (CL-48) was commissioned in 1938 and was lightly damaged during the Japanese attack on Pearl Harbor. HONOLULU suffered at least two additional torpedo strikes during the course of the war. HONOLULU was scrapped after the war — in part due to the structural damage caused by the torpedo hits. She is camouflaged in Measure 32/2C.

USS BIRMINGHAM (CL-62) led an eventful life. Commissioned in 1943, she was hit by bombs and torpedoes in 1943, suffered severe blast damage and casualties while fighting fires on board the light carrier USS PRINCETON in 1944, and was hit by a kamikaze off Okinawa in 1945. Her camouflage scheme — Measure 33/6D — was heavily scorched on the starboard side following the explosion on the PRINCETON.

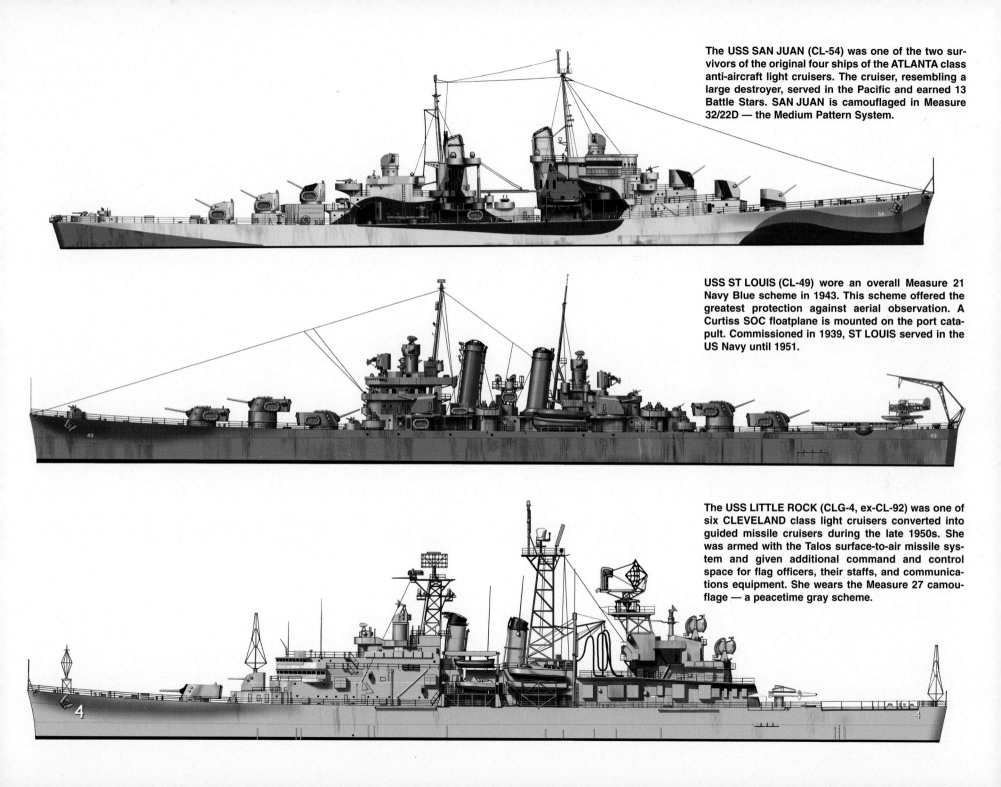

The USS SAN JUAN (CL-54) was one of the two survivors of the original four ships of the ATLANTA class anti-aircraft light cruisers. The cruiser, resembling a large destroyer, served in the Pacific and earned 13 Battle Stars. SAN JUAN is camouflaged in Measure 32/22D — the Medium Pattern System.

USS ST LOUIS (CL-49) wore an overall Measure 21 Navy Blue scheme in 1943. This scheme offered the greatest protection against aerial observation. A Curtiss SOC floatplane is mounted on the port catapult. Commissioned in 1939, ST LOUIS served in the US Navy until 1951.

The USS LITTLE ROCK (CLG-4, ex-CL-92) was one of six CLEVELAND class light cruisers converted into guided missile cruisers during the late 1950s. She was armed with the Talos surface-to-air missile system and given additional command and control space for flag officers, their staffs, and communications equipment. She wears the Measure 27 camouflage — a peacetime gray scheme.

ATLANTA Class

The ATLANTA-OAKLAND class were the smallest and most lightly armed and armored US cruisers ordered since the turn of the century. When the final design was approved by Bureau of Construction and Repair (later designated as BuShips) the new class resembled a large destroyer, but with increased armament. The class was originally designated ATLANTA, but OAKLAND was added to encompass the later and differently configured members.

The ATLANTA class were 541 feet (164.9 M) long and 52 feet 10 inches (16.1 M) in beam. Draft was rated at 20 feet (6.10 M) full load. The ATLANTA displaced a standard 6718 tons (6094.6 MT) and 8340 tons (7566 MT) at her full war load. The four Babcock and Wilcox boilers provided 75,000 shaft horsepower to the two shaft Westinghouse geared turbines. The ATLANTA-OAKLAND class were the only US cruisers to have two screws in WW II. Their speed was rated at 33 knots, although the class was originally designed for 40 knots. Their range amounted to 4000 miles (6437.2 KM) at 25 knots using 1528 tons (1386.2 MT) of onboard fuel. A single 250 Kw generator was fitted for emergency power. A second emergency generator was fitted when the need was shown for additional electric power.

ATLANTA's original 1938 design called for the installation of nine 6-inch/47 guns and a secondary armament of six 5-inch/25 guns for anti-aircraft protection. When the first four ATLANTA class cruisers (CL-51-54) were ordered, the armament had been changed to 16 5-inch/38 dual purpose guns in eight mounts— six on the centerline and two on the main deck at either side of the aft superstructure. These side mounts were designated waist turrets. Four of the new, four barrel 1.1-inch anti-aircraft machine guns were also fitted for close-in AA defense. The expensive and troublesome 1.1-inch 'Chicago Piano' proved to be less than adequate and was replaced once sufficient numbers of Bofors 40 MM AA weapons became available. Additional close-in protection was provided by water-cooled .50 caliber machine guns, which in turn, were replaced by Oerlikon 20 MM cannons.

When the second order for four additional ATLANTA class cruisers (CL-95-98) was placed, the two waist turrets and their combined four 5-inch/38 guns were eliminated in favor of additional 20 and 40 MM guns. This armament change resulted in the class being designated the ATLANTA-OAKLAND class. The OAKLAND was the first of the modified ATLANTAs and when she was commissioned in 1943, the ATLANTA had already been sunk in action. Three additional ATLANTA-OAKLAND class cruisers (CL-119-121) were ordered with further modifications to the main armament. The number 2 through 5 turrets were lowered one deck, effectively reducing topweight. These three ATLANTA-OAKLAND class cruisers were completed after the end of World War II.

The ATLANTA class was fitted with eight 21-inch (53.3 CM) torpedo tubes in two launchers. The tubes were placed just forward of the waist 5-inch mounts. In order to reduce topweight — steadily rising due to the proliferation of AA weapons and radars —a decision was made in 1945 to remove the torpedo tubes. Additionally, they were deleted from the design of the last three ships under construction. A pair of depth charge roller racks were placed on the stern and six depth charge throwers, three per side, were also fitted. The ATLANTA class was also fitted with anti-submarine warfare (ASW) gear for underwater detection of submarines.

Armor protection on the ATLANTA class consisted of a 3.5 inch (8.9 CM) side belt, 1.25 inches (3.2 CM) on the deck, 1.25 inches on the turret faces and 2.5 inches (6.4 CM) on the conning tower. Underwater protection consisted of 1.25 inches around the magazines. This armor was designed to protect both the ship's vitals and the crew — 35 officers and 683 sailors.

Main battery fire control was provided by Mark 37 Mod 2 directors — one forward and one aft — high up on the superstructure. The Mark 37 was further fitted with Mark 12 and 22 radar, which augmented the optical sights of the Mark 37 director. The 1.1-inch and 40 MM anti-aircraft guns were directed by the Mark 51/52 gun director.

When they became available, both air and sea search radars were fitted. The SK or SC radar was placed atop the foremast on the ATLANTAs (CL-51-54). These radars were fitted to both the fore or main mast in the OAKLANDs (CL-95-98). Surface coverage was provided by the SG or SG-1 radar mounted on the fore and main masts. BK/BL Identification Friend or Foe antennas were placed on the fore and mainmast yards.

Three builders constructed the ATLANTA class light cruisers. Federal Shipbuilding, Kearny, New Jersey constructed the ATLANTA (CL-51) and JUNEAU (CL-52). Bethlehem Steel of Quincy, Massachusetts constructed the SAN DIEGO (CL-53) and SAN JUAN (CL-54), while Bethlehem Steel of San Francisco, California built the OAKLAND (CL-95), RENO (CL-96), FLINT (CL-97, ex-SPOKANE), and TUCSON (CL-98). Federal Shipbuilding also built the new JUNEAU (CL-119), SPOKANE (CL-120), and FRESNO (CL-121), although these vessels did not see service in WW II. Each of the ships cost an estimated 15.5 million US dollars.

The combat careers of both ATLANTA (CL-51) and JUNEAU (CL-52) were brief. Both ships were lost during the Battle of Guadalcanal on 13 November 1942. The ATLANTA was the first to feel the guns of the Japanese fleet. The Japanese battleships HIEI and KIRISHIMA were able to hit the ATLANTA over 50 times with their 14-inch guns. A torpedo from a unknown source also found its mark. The ATLANTA went to the bottom of Savo Sound taking over 172 sailors with her.

The JUNEAU also took a torpedo hit and was forced to withdraw . Down by the bow and limping on one screw, the Japanese submarine I-26 put a single torpedo into the JUNEAU. The cruiser broke in two and sank immediately taking 700 sailors to the bottom. The casualties included the five Sullivan brothers who wanted to serve together aboard the JUNEAU. The Sullivan Brothers were later honored by having a FLETCHER class destroyer THE SULLIVANS (DD-537) named for them. Both the HIEI and KIRISHIMA were later lost during the

The ATLANTA (CL-51) rests on the builders ways at Federal Shipbuilding, Kearny, New Jersey prior to her launching on 6 September 1941. The ATLANTA class were the only modern US light cruisers with two screws — all others had four. (Floating Drydock)

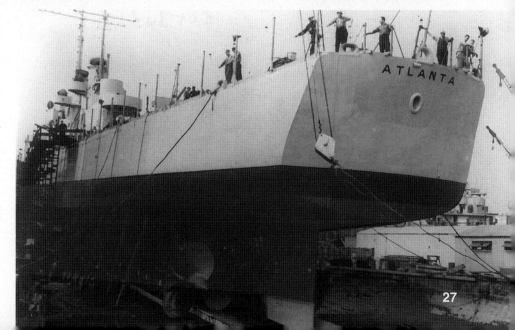

three-day running battle. The ATLANTA was awarded five Battle Stars for her actions and the Presidential Unit Citation for her bravery and gallantry during the Battle of Guadalcanal. The JUNEAU was awarded four Battle Stars.

The ATLANTA class cruisers were redesignated anti-aircraft cruisers and classified CL(AA) in 1949. The class was subdivided into three classes by 1950. The two surviving members of the ATLANTA class were redesignated the SAN DIEGO class. The OAKLAND was designated the class leader of the second build which included three additional ships. The new JUNEAU was the class leader of the last three ships, none of which were completed in time to see service during the war.

The SAN DIEGO (CL-53) earned the most Battle Stars of all the ATLANTA class with 15 to her credit. She was closely followed by SAN JUAN with 13. OAKLAND was awarded nine, FLINT four, RENO three, and TUCSON one.

The ATLANTAs excelled in their designed purpose: provide anti-aircraft support to the US carriers and fast battleships while they fought their way from the South Pacific to Japan.

5-inch/38 Dual Purpose Mount

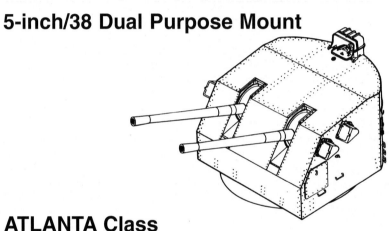

ATLANTA Class

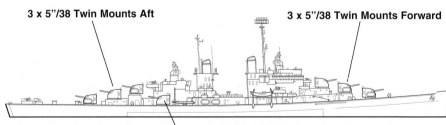

3 x 5"/38 Twin Mounts Aft   3 x 5"/38 Twin Mounts Forward

2 x 5"/38 Twin Mounts in Waist Positions (P&S)

The ATLANTA is moored at dockside on 1 December 1941, just prior to her commissioning. The ATLANTA underwent a brief training period and was sent to the Pacific where she participated in the decisive Battle of Midway. The ATLANTA is camouflaged in Measure 3. (Floating Drydock)

(Above) The ATLANTA conducted her sea trials in the Atlantic off Rockland, Maine during the fall of 1941. Although the ATLANTA class cruisers were designed for 40 knots, they never quite achieved that speed. The ATLANTA was designed to be an anti-aircraft cruiser (CLAA) and armed with sixteen 5-inch/38 dual purpose guns in eight enclosed mounts. (Floating Drydock)

(Right) The JUNEAU (CL-52) cruises slowly off the Atlantic coast on 11 February 1942 — a few days before her commissioning. The JUNEAU is camouflaged in Measure 12 with splotches, although the pattern is markedly different from that of the ATLANTA. The JUNEAU earned four Battle Stars during her brief career in the Pacific. (Real War Photos)

(Below) The ATLANTA was part of the escort screen for the aircraft carrier HORNET (CV-8) and the heavy cruiser NEW ORLEANS (CA-32) during the Battle of Midway. All of these ships were assigned to Task Force 16. The ATLANTA is camouflaged in Measure 12 with splotches. The HORNET was sunk on 26 October 1942 during the Battle of Santa Cruz. The ATLANTA earned five Battle Stars for her actions in the Pacific before she was lost off Guadalcanal on 13 November 1942 — less than three weeks later. NEW ORLEANS survived the war. (Real War Photos)

29

(Above) The JUNEAU shows her fantail after departing Kearny, New Jersey in February of 1942. JUNEAU carries no search radars on her masts, although two of her MK-37 fire control directors are both radar and optically controlled. The JUNEAU is fitted with eight single mount 20 MM weapons for close-in defense. The 1.1-inch anti-aircraft gun, located between the number six 5-inch mount and the after MK-37 gun director, is covered with dark canvas. (Floating Drydock)

(Below) A shore party of the SAN DIEGO (CL-53) prepares to launch a 26-foot (7.9 M) motor launch for a much needed shore leave in 1942. The SAN DIEGO is camouflaged in Measure 12 with splotches. The foremast carries SG radar, while the MK-37 gun director is fitted with a MK-12 radar. The SAN DIEGO earned 15 Battle Stars during her three years of service in the Pacific. This was the most Battle Stars won by any of the ATLANTA Class cruisers. (Floating Drydock)

(Above) A 40 MM anti-aircraft gun crew stands at ready aboard the JUNEAU in 1942. The 40 MM required a minimum crew of seven. Four-round clips of 40 MM ammunition have been placed in the breeches of the guns. The Swedish designed Bofors 40 MM gun had a firing rate of 130 rounds per minute, and could fire high explosive, armor piercing, and tracer rounds. The crew men seated beside the guns turned wheels to traverse and elevate the 40 MM weapons. The life rafts placed starboard of the 40 MM twin mount contains sea survival supplies and equipment. A Mk-52 gun director is situated in the foreground. (Floating Drydock)

(Right) JUNEAU's AA gun crews continue their watch in 1942. Four-round clips of 40 MM ammunition line the interior walls of the 40 MM gun tub. A 40 MM gun crew consisted of a gun captain, a pointer, a trainer, two first loaders and two second loaders. Foot pedals near the seats beside the 40 MM gun mounts were used by gun crews to fire their weapons. The 40 MM gun was originally designed by Bofors of Sweden and licensed produced in the United States. The 20 MM gun was usually manned by a crew of three. A 60 round ammunition drum is clipped to the 20 MM gun. Oerlikon of Switzerland designed the 20 MM weapon, which was produced under license in the US. (Floating Drydock)

'Somewhere in the Pacific', the SAN JUAN (CL-54) rides at anchor in October of 1942. The SAN JUAN is camouflaged in yet another interpretation of Measure 12 with splotches. The SAN JUAN spent her entire career in the Pacific with various task forces and earned 13 Battle Stars. This total is second only to the SAN DIEGO's 15 Battle Stars among the ATLANTAs. Like the SAN DIEGO, the SAN JUAN was built at Bethlehem Steel in Quincy, Massachusetts. (Floating Drydock)

Anti-Aircraft Gun Development

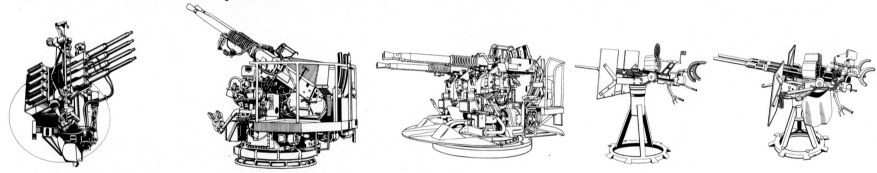

1.1-inch Machine Cannon **40mm Bofors Twin Mount** **40mm Bofors Quad Mount** **20mm Single Mount** **20mm Twin Mount**

The SAN JUAN, moored in San Francisco Bay on 14 October 1944, wears a Measure 33/22D camouflage characterized by broad wavy bands of color. The colors used were Light Gray (5-L), Ocean Gray (5-O), and Black. SAN JUAN carries an SG-1 sea search radar atop her mainmast. An additional SG-1 was placed on top of her foremast. A large SC air search radar antenna is fitted to the main mast. A MK-22 fire control radar has been fitted to the side of the MK-12 fire control radar on the MK-37 gun director. (Floating Drydock)

The OAKLAND (CL-95) represented a modified version of the earlier ships in the ATLANTA class. The OAKLAND — and the six ships which followed — had the waist mounted twin 5-inch guns deleted, an increased 20 MM anti-aircraft armament, and improved gun directors. The ATLANTA class would become the ATLANTA-OAKLAND class following the loss of the ATLANTA in 1942. The OAKLAND is camouflaged in the Measure 21 Navy Blue System. (Floating Drydock)

The FLINT (CL-97) rides at anchor in San Francisco Bay just prior to her commissioning. The FLINT, like her earlier sister ship SAN JUAN, carries Measure 33/22D. These were the only light cruisers to carry that particular scheme. The fore mast on the FLINT contains SC air search and SG-1 sea search radar. The FLINT was originally named the SPOKANE, however, that name was re-allocated to CL-120. (Floating Drydock)

The RENO (CL-96) moves out of San Francisco Bay in 1944 and heads for the Pacific area. The RENO is camouflaged in Measure 31a/24d, a low contrast scheme. Oversize 'bloomers' have been added to the 5-inch turrets in an attempt to keep them dry during foul weather. The tub mounted at the bow above the anchors housed 20 MM anti-aircraft guns. The RENO received three Battle Stars for her actions in the Pacific. (Floating Drydock)

33

(Above) The FLINT (CL-97) entered combat soon after her commissioning on 31 August 1944. The FLINT is camouflaged in Measure 33/22d, a Measure which was wavy on the starboard side and arrowhead shaped to port. Three of the ship's six 5-inch/38 twin-gun turrets are mounted before the superstructure, while the other three are located aft. Additional 20 MM and 40 MM anti-aircraft guns replaced the two waist 5-inch turrets on the last seven ATLANTA-OAKLAND class cruisers. (Real War Photos)

(Below) The FLINT's crew mill about the deck while the ship is slowly underway. During the course of the war, the secondary 20 MM and 40 MM AA armament on most US Navy ships serving in the Pacific was steadily increased. The ATLANTA-OAKLAND class cruisers were the only light cruisers not to be equipped with catapults or an aircraft-handling crane. The class could carry one floatplane in lieu of a ship's boat, however, this capability was not used. The FLINT earned four Battle Stars while serving in the Pacific. (Floating Drydock)

(Below) The FLINT was fitted out at a busy Bethlehem Shipyard wharf in San Francisco during early 1945. She served as a floating AA battery off the coast of Japan during the war's final months. Following the war, the FLINT was reclassified as a CLAA (anti-aircraft light cruiser) and served in the Pacific Fleet until 1966. (Floating Drydock)

(Above) Following her commissioning on 3 February 1945, the TUCSON (CL-98) was sent to the Pacific for crew training and workup prior to the planned invasion of Japan. TUCSON was awarded one Battle Star for her actions off Japan. The TUCSON is camouflaged in Measure 21, the Navy Blue System. (Floating Drydock)

(Below) The SPOKANE (CL-120) rides high in the water following her launching on 22 September 1945. Too late to serve during the war, she served in the Pacific Reserve fleet until decommissioned in 1949. SPOKANE was later recommissioned as a test ship designated AG-191. She was broken up in 1973. (Real War Photos)

35

CLEVELAND Class

The CLEVELAND class represented the largest build of any single class of light cruisers during the Second World War. A total of 29 were built and 22 of these served during the war. A further nine hulls, laid down as cruisers, were converted into INDEPENDENCE class light carriers (CVL).

The US Navy, knowing the long lead time between the design and launching of a new ship class, decided to improve the older BROOKLYNs rather than design a whole new class of ships. Consequently, the CLEVELANDs were upgraded BROOKLYN and ST LOUIS class cruisers — or more specifically, the HELENA. They shared similar dimensions and outward appearances, however the CLEVELANDs had one less 6-inch main battery turret, but four more 5-inch anti-aircraft guns. The CLEVELAND (CL 55) was laid down on 1 July 1940 and launched on 1 November 1941. Her cost was estimated at over 31 million US dollars.

The CLEVELAND was 608 feet, 4 inches (185.4 M) long overall and 600 feet (182.9 M) at the waterline. Her beam was 63 feet (19.2 M) and she had a 23-foot (7 M) draft. The hulls were similar to the earlier ST LOUIS class, however, the hull sloped inward (known as a tumble home) at the top amidships and the stern was rounded off.

The CLEVELAND class was armed with twelve 6-inch/47 Mk 16 guns in four turrets — two forward and two aft. The 6-inch guns had a range of 26,100 yards (23,865.8 M) using armor piercing ammunition. Her secondary armament consisted of twelve 5-inch/38 dual-purpose guns paired in six Mk 32 mounts. The 5-inch guns had a range of 18,000 yards (16,459.2 M). Additional anti-aircraft protection was provided by a variety of 40 MM Bofors and 20 MM Oerlikon guns — usually twenty-eight 40 MM in twin and quad mounts and twenty 20 MM in single and dual mounts, although this did sometimes vary from ship to ship. This weapons suite, combined with her armor protection, provided optimum anti-aircraft protection. No CLEVELAND class light cruiser was lost to enemy action.

The CLEVELANDs were powered by four Babcock and Wilcox high pressure, high temperature boilers which provided over 100,000 shaft horsepower to the four General Electric geared turbines. The boiler and engine rooms were staggered as in the ST LOUIS class. Four screws provided a speed of up to 33 knots. The onboard 2409 tons (2185.4 MT) of fuel oil provided a range of 5600 miles (9012 KM) at 25 knots. Two 250 Kw diesel-electric generators provided emergency power in case boiler pressure was lost.

All of the CLEVELANDs had two funnels except the last two class members — FARGO (CL 106) and HUNTINGTON (CL 107). These ships used a single funnel located between the main and foremast. Both of these cruisers were completed too late to see service during the war.

Armor protection consisted of a 5-inch (12.7 CM) thick, 400 foot (121.9 M) long belt along the hull side. The deck was given 2 inches (5 CM), while the bulkheads were provided with 5 inches. The turrets were faced with 6.5 inches (16.5 CM), with 3 inches (7.6 CM) on the roof and 3 inches on the side. The conning tower was armored with 5 inches on the side and 2.5 inches (6.3 CM) on the roof. The increased armor raised the CLEVELAND's displacement to 11,700 tons (10,614.2 MT) standard and 14,400 tons (13,063.7 MT) at full war load. This was a considerable increase over the earlier BROOKLYNs. In fact, the CLEVELANDs were widely regarded as being overweight and somewhat unstable — a feeling that was only exacerbated by the fitting of additional weapons and electronic gear as the war progressed.

The CLEVELANDS, in concert with the earlier BROOKLYNS, were given two aircraft cat-

BROOKLYN Class

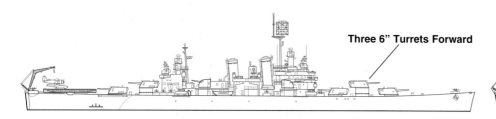

Three 6" Turrets Forward

The CLEVELAND (CL-55) was authorized in 1939 and laid down in 1940. The CLEVELAND class were the most numerous of any cruiser class of World War Two. Of the 29 CLEVELANDs constructed, 22 served in the war. The CLEVELAND, seen here on 19 July

CLEVELAND Class

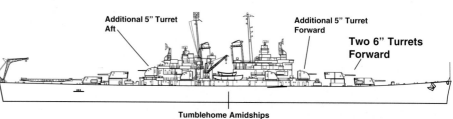

Additional 5" Turret Aft

Additional 5" Turret Forward

Two 6" Turrets Forward

Tumblehome Amidships

1942 at Philadelphia Navy Yard, is camouflaged in Measure 12 with splotches. The CLEVELAND was armed with twelve 6-inch/47caliber guns mounted in four turrets. (Floating Drydock)

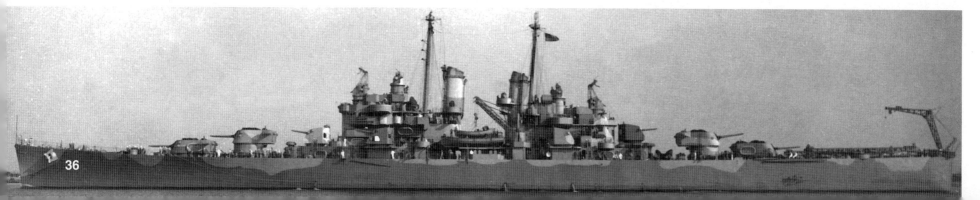

apults, a single aircraft/cargo handling crane, and a below deck hangar on the fantail. The CLEVELANDs could handle up to eight aircraft — two on the catapults and six in the hangar. The normal aircraft complement was four, usually OS2U Kingfishers or SOC Seagulls.

Two other aircraft served aboard the CLEVELANDs: the SO3C Seamew (a name sure to strike fear in the hearts of the enemy) and SC-1 Seahawk, both built by Curtiss. The SO3C proved to be completely inadequate for shipboard service, while the Seahawk came too late in the war to see much service. By 1945, it was decided to reduce top weight by removing one of the two catapults. This modification was actually completed on the CLEVELAND (CL 55), ATLANTA (CL 104), and HUNTINGTON (CL 107), all of which had their starboard catapults beached.

The CLEVELAND class was provided with extensive radio, radar, and electronic equipment. The main 6-inch battery was controlled by Mark 34 gun directors with Mark 8 antennas on the director roof. Two directors were fitted high on the fore and aft superstructures. The Mark 34 director was also fitted with a stereoscopic range finder and spotting telescopes to locate targets. The director crew was protected by a 1-inch (2.54 CM) thick shield.

The Mark 37 director was used for the 5-inch guns. This director was fitted with Mk12 radar. Later, the Mk 22 radar was added to provide altitude ranging. The 40 MM Bofors were controlled by the Mark 51 gun director with an attached Mark 14 electric sight. The Mark 51 could automatically direct the 40 MM weapons to their target. The Mark 51 directors were mounted on bandstands in the area of the twin funnels.

Four air and sea search radar antennas were fitted to the tops of the main and foremasts. The square SC/SK antennas and sets were used for air search (the SC was a smaller version of the SK). The circular SK-2 was an upgraded antenna that replaced the SC/SK later in the war. Sea search radars included the SG and later SG-16 antennas and sets. There were usually two SG antennas mounted — one each on the main and foremast — to ensure complete sea coverage. A few ships, notably the BIRMINGHAM (CL 62) and ATLANTA (CL 104), were fitted with SL or SU radar.

During the first year of the Pacific War, the US Navy lost eight cruisers: two light and six heavies. The CLEVELAND and her sisters began arriving just in time to fill the void left by these losses. The 22 CLEVELANDs earned a total of 132 Battle Stars for their actions during World War II — most of them in the Pacific Theatre. CLEVELAND (CL 55), COLUMBIA (CL 56), MONTPELIER (CL 57), DENVER (CL 58), SANTA FE (CL 60), and BIRMINGHAM (CL 62) were all awarded the Navy Unit Commendation for their service and bravery of their crews during the many battles of their three-year career. The TOPEKA (CLG 8) was awarded three Battle Stars and OKLAHOMA CITY (CLG 5) 12 Battle Stars for their service during the Vietnam War, both as Guided Missile Cruisers.

By 1950, all of the CLEVELAND class light cruisers, with the exception of the MANCHESTER (CL 83) serving with the Pacific Active Fleet, were put into Pacific and Atlantic Reserve Fleets. By 1965 only nine remained in the Reserve Fleet, the balance of 20 were either scrapped, expended as targets, or converted to Guided Missile Cruisers (CLG). Six of the CLEVELAND class were converted to CLGs: GALVESTON (CL 93), LITTLE ROCK (CL 92), OKLAHOMA CITY (CL 91), PROVIDENCE (CL 82), SPRINGFIELD (CL 66), and TOPEKA (CL 67).

SK and SG radar are fitted to the foremast and SG radar mounted atop the mainmast of the CLEVELAND. The CLEVELAND had earned 13 Battle Stars for her exploits in the both the Atlantic and Pacific by the end of the World War Two. The CLEVELAND is camouflaged in Measure 22 in this 1945 photo. (Elsilrac)

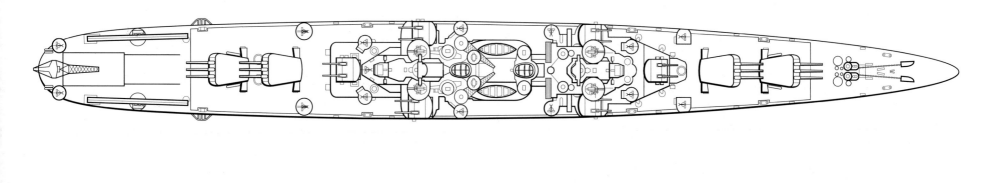

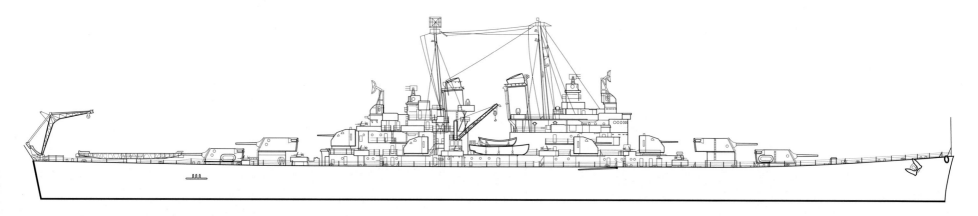

CLEVELAND Class Light Cruiser

Length:....................608 Feet, 4 Inches
Beam:......................63 Feet
Draught:...................23 Feet
Displacement:.........11,700 Tons Standard, 14,400 Tons Full
                  Load
Propulsion:.............100,000 shp/Four Screws
Speed:....................33 Knots
Complement:..........1,356

Armament:..................12 x 6-inch/47 Guns in Four Turrets,
6 x Twin 5-inch/38 Turrets, 28 x 40 mm
Bofors in Twin/Quad Mounts, 20 x
20 mm Oerlikon in Single/Twin
Mounts.
Aircraft:......................2-4 x OS2U or SOC/SON Floatplanes
(up to eight could be carried)

The SANTA FE (CL-60) accompanies an escort carrier and a NORTH CAROLINA class battleship in the Pacific in 1945. The cruiser is camouflaged in Measure 21, the Navy Blue scheme. SG sea search radars are installed on top of the foremast and mainmast. The SANTA FE was awarded the Navy Commendation Medal and 13 Battle Stars for her heroic actions during World War Two. (Floating Drydock)

The BIRMINGHAM (CL-62) returns from a refit following a torpedo and bomb attack which damaged her in 1943. Camouflaged in Measure 33/6D, she steams in the Pacific in 1944 looking for a fight and revenge. The BIRMINGHAM earned nine Battle Stars and the Navy Unit Commendation for her service in both the Atlantic and Pacific during World War Two. (Floating Drydock)

MONTPELIER (CL-57) enters the ASBD-1 floating drydock for some much needed hull repairs in 1944. She is camouflaged in Measure 22 — Navy Blue (5-N) and Haze Gray (5-H). This scheme would soon be changed to Measure 32/11A. The MONTPELIER earned 13 Battle Stars during her three year Pacific campaign. (Real War Photos)

The BIRMINGHAM shows the scars and blistered paint after fighting the fires aboard the light carrier PRINCETON (CVL-23) during the Battle of Leyte Gulf on 24 October 1944. The BIRMINGHAM was along side the carrier when the PRINCETON suddenly exploded killing 237 and wounding 426 members of her crew. Following her repairs the BIRMINGHAM returned to the Pacific, only to be hit by a kamikaze off Okinawa and put out of action for the remainder of the war. (Real War Photos)

(Above) The PASADENA (CL-65), wearing a Measure 32/24D camouflage, cruises in calm Pacific waters in July of 1944. A pair of Vought-Sikorsky OS2U-3 float planes from VCS-17 are stowed on the catapults. CLEVELAND class cruisers had a normal compliment of four aircraft, however, up to eight aircraft — two on the catapults and six in the stern hangar — could be accommodated. The PASADENA was awarded five Battle Stars for her ten months of service in the Pacific. (Real War Photos)

(Below) The SPRINGFIELD (CL-66) is barely underway in Boston Harbor on 8 September 1944. The SPRINGFIELD was commissioned in September of 1944 and joined the fight in the Pacific just in time for the invasion of Okinawa. She earned two Battle Stars for her abbreviated tour in the Pacific. Following the war she was converted to a guided missile cruiser (CLG-7) — a conversion which drastically altered her appearance. SPRINGFIELD is wearing a Measure 33/24D camouflage scheme. (Floating Drydock)

(Floating Drydock)

Radars and Gun Directors

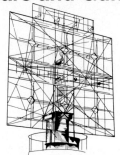

SK Radar

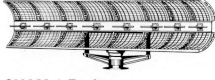

CXAM-1 Radar

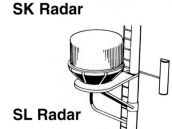

SL Radar

SU Radar

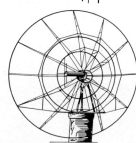

SK-2 Radar

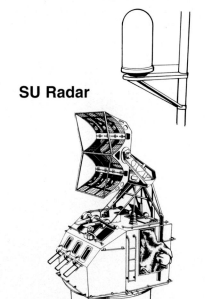

Mk 37 Director

The HOUSTON (CL-81, originally VICKSBURG) was renamed for the sunken heavy cruiser HOUSTON (CA-30) after the citizens of Houston, Texas pledged War Bond money for her construction costs. The original HOUSTON was lost during the Battle of the Java Sea on 1 March 1942. The new HOUSTON was awarded three Battle Stars for her Pacific actions. The ship is camouflaged in Measure 32/1D. Five-inch/38 twin-gun turrets are mounted immediately fore and aft of the superstructure. (Floating Drydock)

The VICKSBURG (CL-86), originally the CHEYENNE, was renamed before her launching on 14 December 1943. She entered combat in 1945 off Iwo Jima following crew training. The VICKSBURG is camouflaged in Measure 33/6D and carries SK and SG search radars on her mast tops. The 6-inch/47 guns of VICKSBURG and her sisters had a range of 26,100 yards (23,865.8 м) using armor piercing ammunition. These guns were mounted in four triple turrets, two forward and two aft of the superstructure. (Floating Drydock)

The MIAMI (CL-89) rides a light chop while at anchor in San Pedro, California on 18 July 1945. A pair of Curtiss SC-1 Sea Hawk scout planes from VCS-14 sit on the catapults. The aircraft handling crane has been folded forward between the catapults. The MIAMI is camouflaged in Measure 22, the Graded System. The MIAMI was awarded six Battle Stars for her one-year career in the Pacific. (Floating Drydock)

The HOUSTON's damage control party jettisons the starboard aircraft catapult off the stern following the hit by a second torpedo. The damaged port catapult and OS2U Kingfisher will also be 'deep sixed'. The heroic actions of the damage control parties and crew saved the HOUSTON from sinking. She was not repaired in time to finish out the war. (Real War Photos)

The ASTORIA (CL-90) moves slowly out of Mare Island, California on 21 October 1944. Originally named WILKES-BARRE, the ASTORIA was renamed for the heavy cruiser ASTORIA (CA-34) that was lost during the Battle of Savo Island on 9 August 1942. The ASTORIA is camouflaged in Measure 33/24D. A pair of OS2U Kingfishers assigned to VCS-17 are stowed on the catapults. (Floating Drydock)

The HOUSTON eases into a drydock to repair stern damage caused by an aerial torpedo off Formosa on 14 October 1944. While under tow by the tug PAWNEE (ATF-74), the HOUSTON was hit by another aerial torpedo. Although in danger of sinking, the ship's crew saved the foundering cruiser. The HOUSTON wears Measure 32/1D. (Floating Drydock)

(Above) The OKLAHOMA CITY (CL-91) rests at Philadelphia Navy yard on 9 April 1945. An SC-1 Seahawk from VCS-20 sits on the swung out port catapult. She wears a Measure 22 paint scheme. The OKLAHOMA CITY was awarded two Battle Stars for her three months' service during World War Two. She would earn 12 more Battle Stars for her actions off Vietnam as a Guided Missile Cruiser (CLG-5) just over twenty years later. (Floating Drydock)

(Below) The AMSTERDAM (CL-101) awaits orders on 29 January 1945 shortly after her commissioning ceremonies at Newport News, Virginia. A Mark 34 director for the 6-inch main guns is mounted above the bridge. Above and aft of the Mark 34 is the Mark 37 director for the 5-inch guns. She earned one Battle Star for her actions off Japan during the closing days of the Pacific War. The AMSTERDAM is camouflaged in Measure 31A/10C. (Floating Drydock)

The WILKES-BARRE (CL-103), floating in the calm waters of Philadelphia Navy Yard, is camouflaged in Measure 32/24D on 18 August 1944. The gun openings on the main turrets are fitted with 'bloomers' to keep the elements out of the turret interior. She earned four Battle Stars for her service in the Pacific from January to August of 1945. The WILKES-BARRE was placed in the Reserve Fleet in 1947. She remained in reserve until she was sacrificed to Navy tests in the Atlantic in 1972. (Floating Drydock)

Cruiser Floatplanes

Curtiss SOC-3 Seagull **Vought OS2U Kingfisher** **Curtiss SO3C Seamew** **Curtiss SC-1 Seahawk**

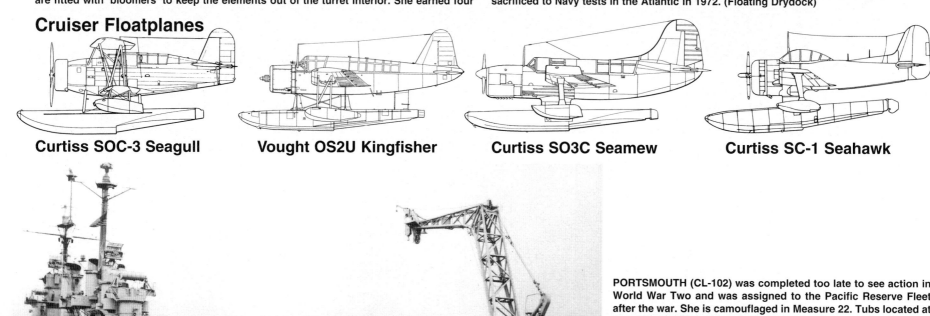

PORTSMOUTH (CL-102) was completed too late to see action in World War Two and was assigned to the Pacific Reserve Fleet after the war. She is camouflaged in Measure 22. Tubs located at the stern flanking the crane house twin 40 MM antiaircraft guns. The CLEVELAND class cruisers usually carried 28 40 MM guns in both twin and quad mounts. This number sometimes varied from ship to ship. Waste water from the ship's bilges flows from openings in the hull just above the waterline. The framework above and forward of the rearmost bilge opening is a propeller guard. This guard is mounted to protect crewmen and objects falling off the deck from striking the ship's forward propellers. Following her service in the Reserve Fleet, PORTSMOUTH was stricken and sold for scrap in 1970. (Floating Drydock)

(Above) The ATLANTA (CL-104) was named for the light cruiser ATLANTA (CL-51) — lost during the Battle of Guadalcanal in November of 1942. She was awarded two Battle Stars during the closing months of the Pacific war. The ATLANTA carries a single Curtiss SC-1 scout plane from VO-15C on her port catapult. The ATLANTA, seen here in 1947, is camouflaged in Measure 27, an overall light gray scheme worn by US Navy ships in peacetime. (Floating Drydock)

(Right) The HUNTINGTON (CL-107), when completed in 1944, was originally considered a part of the CLEVELAND class. Following the war, she and her sister ship (and class leader) FARGO (CL-106) were placed into a separate class to recognize the differences from their earlier sisters. The major difference was in the single large stack versus the thinner twin stacks in the CLEVELANDs. An SC-1 Seahawk is mounted on the port catapult. (Floating Drydock)

The WILKES-BARRE, wearing Measure 32/24D camouflage, cuts through calm waters in September of 1944. A pair of Naval Aircraft Factory OS2N-1 Kingfisher scout planes from Cruiser Scouting Division Seventeen (VCS-17) are stowed on the catapults. The OS2N-1 was the designation given to Vought OS2U-3s constructed by the Naval Aircraft Factory in Philadelphia during 1942. (Floating Drydock)

WORCESTER Class

The WORCESTER class cruisers were built to mount the new 6-inch/47 dual-purpose gun. Only two ships were built — WORCESTER (CL-144) and ROANOKE (CL-145). Two additional ships, VALLEJO (CL-146) and GARY (CL-147), were cancelled on 11 August 1945, two days after the atomic bomb was dropped on Nagasaki.

The WORCESTER class was 679 feet, 6 inches (207.1 M) long overall and 664 feet (202.4 M) at the waterline. Their beam was 70 feet, 8 inches (21.5 M) and they had a mean draft of 25 feet (7.62 M) at full war load. Displacement was rated at 14,700 tons (13,335.8 MT) standard and 18,500 tons (16,783.2 MT) at full war load. Their displacement put the WORCESTERs into the displacement class of the BALTIMORE (CA-68) class heavy cruisers.

The WORCESTER class was powered by four Babcock and Wilcox boilers which provided 120,000 shaft horsepower to the four General Electric geared turbines. There were four boiler rooms and two engine rooms. The boiler and engine rooms were staggered — a design element carried over from the earlier CLEVELANDs. The four screws provided a speed of up to 33 knots. The WORCESTER's 2400 tons (2177.3 MT) of onboard fuel provided a range of 8000 miles (12,874.4 KM) at 15 knots.

The WORCESTER class was originally envisioned as having a 6-inch (15.24 CM) armored deck and no 5-inch anti-aircraft guns. This exceptionally thick armored deck, along with the 6-inch dual purpose guns, was designed to defeat bombs and missiles launched from high altitude bombers. As built, the deck was armored with 3.5 inches (8.9 CM) and the belt, along the ship's most vulnerable areas, was 5 inches (12.7 CM) thick. The turrets were faced with 6.5 inches (16.5 CM) with 4 inches (10.2 CM) on the roof, 3 inches (7.62 CM) on the sides, and 5 inches on the barbettes. All of this steel armor plating was designed to protect the 1401 members of the crew and the ship's guns, magazines, and engineering spaces.

The WORCESTER class was armed with twelve 6-inch/47 (152 MM) Mark 16 automatic, dual-purpose guns in six turrets. The 6-inch gun could fire two different types of ammunition—armor piercing (AP) and proximity fused anti-aircraft (AAA) rounds. Each gun was provided with separate hoists for surface (AP) or air targets (AAA). Secondary anti-aircraft protection was originally comprised of forty-eight 40 MM Bofors cannons (44 in 11 quad mounts and four in two twin mounts) and twenty 20 MM Oerlikon guns in single mounts. This secondary anti-

aircraft armament was changed to twenty-four 3-inch/50 Mark 22 rapid fire (RF) guns in 11 twin mounts and two single mounts. The single mount 3-inch RF weapons were mounted on the fantail and radar controlled. All 20 MM weapons were later changed to 12 twin mounts.

The 6-inch main battery was controlled by Mark 37 directors with roof mounted Mark 28 radar. The Mark 37 was originally designed to control the 5-inch dual purpose guns on earlier light cruisers, but was adapted for use on the WORCESTERs. Mark 13 radar was used for surface fire control, while Mark 56 radar was used for the 3-inch guns.

An air search radar capability was provided by the SR-6 system mounted on the second funnel and an SPS-8 height finder radar placed on the main mast. Surface search was provided by an SR-2 radar mounted on the foremast. A Tactical Air Navigation (TACAN) dome was also mounted on the foremast.

When the WORCESTER class were on the builders ways at New York Shipbuilding, aircraft were still being embarked on light cruisers in the war zones. By the time the two ships were launched and commissioned, aircraft were being removed from ships. The WORCESTER and ROANOKE were completed with an aircraft handling crane and hangar at the stern, but no catapults. The fantail was utilized as a boat deck, while the crane was used for boat and bulk cargo handling. The below deck hangar was used as an all-weather storage facility for the boats.

Both WORCESTER and ROANOKE became part of the active Pacific Fleet, serving as Cruiser Divisions flagships until 1958 when they were deactivated and placed in the Reserve Fleet. The WORCESTER served during the Korean Conflict and earned three Battle Stars for her efforts. Both cruisers were stricken and sold for scrap in 1970.

WORCESTER Class

Aircraft Catapults Deleted

6"47 Mk 16 Dual Purpose Guns

3"/50 RF AAA Guns

The WORCESTER (CL-144) was armed with the new automatic, dual purpose 6-inch/47 caliber (152 MM) Mk-16 gun in six twin mounts. Her secondary armament consisted of twenty-four 3-inch/50s in twin mounts and twelve 20 MM cannons for close-in defense. Commissioned on 25 June 1948, she was stricken on 12 January 1970. (Floating Drydock)

The ROANOKE (CL-145) was actually commissioned two months before the WORCESTER. She carried the same armament as her sister and usually served alongside her in fleet service. No catapults were fitted and no aircraft were assigned. Both ships were camouflaged in Measure 27 — an overall peace time gray. (Floating Drydock)

Light Cruiser Conversions

US Navy ships have been the subject of conversions to meet critical needs during the times of both peace and war. One example includes the conversion of World War I flush deck destroyers to mine layers (DM) and minesweepers (DMS). This conversion came about when a need was seen for these types of ships, then lacking in the fleet, and an abundance of available hulls.

A similar need came about at the beginning of the Second World War when the German U-Boats began sinking Allied cargo ships in the Atlantic at an alarming rate. This brought about conversion of C-3 cargo ships to escort carriers (CVE) to accompany Allied convoys plying the Atlantic. By 1944, the U-Boat menace was almost completely eliminated in the Atlantic, thanks in most part to the escort carriers and their escort destroyers (DE).

The escort carrier possessed many disadvantages: small size, slow speed (up to 18 knots), and lack of sufficient armor and armament. The one major advantage was numbers — over 100 escort carriers were built in two years. By comparison, the Japanese built and launched only 10 aircraft carriers of all sizes during the Pacific War with the Allies (7 December 1941 - 2 September 1945).

By the end of 1942, the US Navy had lost four of her eight fleet carriers in the Pacific and did not expect the new ESSEX class (CV-9) to be available until late 1943. Desperate times called for desperate measures and President Franklin Roosevelt directed that nine hulls of the CLEVELAND class light cruisers be converted to light aircraft carriers available for combat by 1943. The conversions, begun in 1942, followed along the lines of the escort carriers. A flight deck and hangar area was placed on the main deck, while an island was located on the starboard side of the flight deck. The islands were of the same design as the CVEs.

The nine new carriers were designated as Light Aircraft Carriers (CVL) and the class leader INDEPENDENCE (CVL-22), ex AMSTERDAM (CL-59), was commissioned on 14 January 1943, a few weeks after the ESSEX. The eight CVLs that followed were the PRINCETON (CVL-23), ex TALLAHASSEE (CL-61); BELLEAU WOOD (CVL-24), ex NEW HAVEN (CL-76); COWPENS (CVL-25), ex HUNTINGTON (CL-77); MONTEREY (CVL-26), ex DAYTON (CL-78); LANGLEY (CVL-27), ex FARGO (CL-85); CABOT (CVL-28), ex WILMINGTON (CL-79); BATAAN (CVL-29), ex BUFFALO (CL-99); and SAN JACINTO (CVL-30), ex NEWARK (CL-100). All of the INDEPENDENCE class carriers were commis-

sioned in 1943. Only the PRINCETON was lost — sunk on 24 October 1944 during the Battle of Leyte Gulf.

The conversion of six CLEVELAND class light cruisers into guided missile cruisers (CLG) began in 1957. The six guided missile cruisers were built in two classes: GALVESTON (CLG-3), ex (CL-93), and PROVIDENCE (CLG-6), ex (CL-82). The GALVESTON class ships were armed with a twin Talos surface to air missile (SAM) system with a capacity of 46 missiles. The PROVIDENCE class was armed with the smaller Terrier SAM system with a capacity of 120 missiles. The primary mission of both classes was fleet air defense. The conversions also led to the removal of most of the 6-inch main battery, the 5-inch secondary battery, and 40 MM and 20 MM AA weapons. The latest radar and countermeasure sets were also installed.

GALVESTON (CLG-3) and TOPEKA (CLG-8) were armed with six 6-inch/47 guns and three twin mounted 5-inch/38 guns — all mounted forward. The remaining four CLGs: LITTLE ROCK (CLG-4), ex (CL-92); OKLAHOMA CITY (CLG-5), ex (CL-91); PROVIDENCE (CLG-6), ex (CL-82); and SPRINGFIELD (CLG-7), ex (CL-66) were armed with three 6-inch/47 and one twin mount 5-inch/38. The 6-inch guns were controlled by the Mark 34 director, while the 5-inch guns were directed by the Mark 37 director fitted with Mark 28 radar.

Both the Talos and Terrier SAM systems were controlled by the Mark 77 integrated missile fire control system. The Mk 77 system consisted of SPS-2, SPS-26, and SPS-29 radars and missile illuminators for the Talos missile system and SPS-8, SPS-26, and SPS-29 for the Terrier missile system. The SPS-2 radar antenna was the largest of the antennas on the CLGs. A TACAN dome antenna was placed atop the fore or main mast, depending on the ship. The GALVESTON class was fitted with two lattice masts, while the PROVIDENCE class cruisers were equipped with three lattice masts.

The LITTLE ROCK, OKLAHOMA CITY, PROVIDENCE, and SPRINGFIELD all became flagships and had enlarged forward superstructures to accommodate flag officers, their staffs, and their additional communications equipment. The OKLAHOMA CITY served as flagship for the Seventh Fleet off Vietnam and earned 13 Battle Stars for her service. The OKLAHOMA CITY remained in service until 1979. The TOPEKA also served off Vietnam and earned three Battle Stars while providing fire support, search and rescue of downed airmen, and fleet defense. Following her tour in Vietnam, the TOPEKA was sent to the Mediterranean, where she served until she was decommissioned in 1969.

The light carrier BATAAN (CVL-29) was the former light cruiser BUFFALO (CL-99). She was one of nine CLEVELAND class light cruisers converted into Light Carriers (CVL) during WW II. The BATAAN served in both WW II and in Korea. BATAAN is carrying F4U Corsairs assigned to Marine Corps Squadron VMF-312 in 1952. (Floating Drydock)

The TOPEKA (CLG-8, ex CL-67) sails out of Pearl Harbor on her way to the shores of Vietnam. The TOPEKA is armed with six 6-inch/47 guns in triple mounts, six 5-inch/38 in twin mounts, and the Terrier Missile system aft. She was awarded two Battle Stars in World War II and three Battle Stars for service in Vietnam. (Elsilrac)

(Above) The LITTLE ROCK (CLG-4, ex CL-92), was converted to a Guided Missile Cruiser and further modified for use as a flagship. The flagship modifications entailed adding an enlarged superstructure to house the increased command and control staff. Main armament was reduced to three 6-inch/47guns in a single mount and one twin 5-inch/38 for use against small surface targets. A twin Talos launcher was mounted on the after deck. (Elsilrac)

(Left) The PROVIDENCE (CLG-6, ex CL-82 and the class leader) was commissioned too late for service in WW II. Her conversion to a Guided Missile Cruiser began at Boston Navy Yard on 1 June 1957. The conversions included the removal of all but one of the triple 6-inch/47 mounts and one of the 5-inch/38 mounts and the addition of the Terrier Missile Systems. The superstructure space was also increased for use by the command and control staff. (Elsilrac)

(Below) The SPRINGFIELD (CLG-7, ex CL-66) was converted to a Guided Missile Cruiser and recommissioned in July of 1960 when she joined the Atlantic Fleet. She was configured as a Flagship with increased superstructure space. The former hangar space was reconfigured to store up to 120 Terrier missiles for the twin launcher. The SPRINGFIELD was awarded two Battle Stars during WW II. (Elsilrac)

Foreign Service

After WW II, all surviving members of the BROOKLYN class and the ST LOUIS were decommissioned and placed in the Reserve Fleet. By 1950, the hulls of all were some 15 years old and been through a war — most sustaining some damage and some sustaining severe damage. A plan to scrap the entire lot was considered. Then the Cold War stepped in.

A decision was made to sell six of the light cruisers through a Military Assistance Program (MAP) to three South American countries in 1950. The decision was made for many reasons, but among them was a desire to keep parity in the three largest navies in South America. Another was to keep South America strong enough to repel any real or perceived enemies — mainly communist — from attacking. Finally, the ships provided a means of paying back Argentina, Brazil, and Chile for their assistance during World War Two.

In January of 1951, five of the BROOKLYNs and the ST LOUIS were sold to Argentina, Brazil, and Chile. Argentina received the PHOENIX (CL-46) and BOISE (CL-47), Brazil acquired the PHILADELPHIA (CL-41) and ST LOUIS (CL-49), and Chile took possession of the BROOKLYN (CL-40) and NASHVILLE (CL-43). The ships were sold at 10 percent of their original cost plus the cost of refurbishing and refitting.

In Argentine service the PHOENIX was renamed the 17 de OCTUBRE and later, the GENERAL BELGRANO. BOISE was renamed the NUEVE de JULIO (NINTH OF JULY). The NUEVE de JULIO served until 1979 when she was decommissioned and sold for breaking up. By 1982, the GENERAL BELGRANO and the VEINTECINCO DE MAYO (the ex-British light fleet carrier VENERABLE) were the two largest ships in the Argentine Navy.

On 2 April 1982, Argentina invaded the Falkland Islands, which the Argentinians called Islas Malvinas, and seized them from a small British garrison. An immediate state of war existed and the British sent their air, naval, and ground forces to reclaim their territory. The British declared a 200-mile (322 KM) 'maritime exclusion zone' around the Falklands in an attempt to keep the Argentinians from building up their forces on the islands. The VEINTECINCO DE MAYO was briefly involved in the invasion, but returned to port shortly thereafter.

The absence of VEINTECINCO DE MAYO left the GENERAL BELGRANO, the most powerful ship in either fleet, to carry her 15 6-inch guns into battle against British air and surface units. GENERAL BELGRANO was also armed with the British-designed Seacat close range surface to air missile system, a weapon known well by the British.

GENERAL BELGRANO had been sailing in and out of the exclusion zone for a few days when she suddenly headed for the British fleet off the Falklands on 2 May 1982. The HMS CONQUEROR, a nuclear powered attack submarine, had been following the GENERAL BELGRANO and flashed a message to the British Chief of Defence Staff that the exclusion zone had been breached and an attempt by the Argentine cruiser to attack the fleet was certain. The message back to the CONQUEROR was to engage and CONQUEROR's commanding officer, Captain Richard Wraith, ordered the launch of a pair of Tigerfish torpedoes. Both torpedoes found their mark on the port side and the GENERAL BELGRANO began taking on water. The damage was so severe that she sank within 20 minutes — taking 358 Argentine sailors to the bottom of the Atlantic. The sinking was the first for a major warship since the end of World War II.

The Brazilian Navy renamed the PHILADELPHIA the BARROSO, and the ST LOUIS the TAMADARE. BARROSO served until 1973 when she was decommissioned and put up for disposal. TAMADARE served to 1975 when she suffered the same fate that most warships must face: scrapping for the metal that can be reused.

The NASHVILLE became the CAPITAN PRAT (later renamed the CHACABUCO) in the Chilean Navy, while the BROOKLYN was renamed the O'HIGGINS (02). The O'HIGGINS began her service with the Chilean Navy in 1951 following a refit that included the removal of both catapults. Additional modifications saw the installation of improved SPS 12 search and SPS 10 tactical radars. The O'HIGGINS served until 1983 when she was decommissioned and put up for disposal. The CHACABUCO served until 1983 when she was decommissioned and placed on the disposal list. In 1985, the CHACABUCO was purchased and towed to Taiwan for scrapping, an event that marked the end of the US Navy's 1930s Treaty Cruisers.

The CHACABUCO (03 and ex-CAPITAN PRAT) was the former BROOKLYN class light cruiser NASHVILLE (CL-43) that was sold to Chile on 9 January 1951. Her configuration, with the exception of the beached catapults, was little changed from her World War Two appearance. The CHACABUCO served with the Chilean Navy until 1983 when she was sold for scrap after serving two navies for over 35 years. (Navy of Chile)

US Fleet Warships from squadron/signal publications

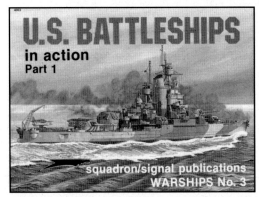

4003 US Battleships in Action pt 1

4004 US Battleships in Action pt 2

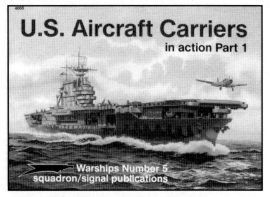

4005 US Aircraft Carriers in Action pt 1

4007 PT Boats in Action

4008 Fletcher DDs in Action

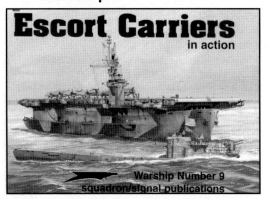

4009 Escort Carriers in Action

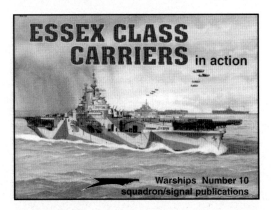

4010 Essex Class Carriers in Action

4011 Destroyer Escorts in Action

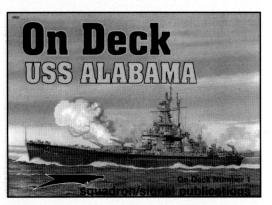

5601 USS Alabama On Deck